D0979276

Bears

An Altitude SuperGuide

Bears

by Kevin Van Tighem

Altitude Publishing
The Canadian Rockies/Vancouver

Publication Information

Altitude Publishing Canada Ltd.
1500 Railway Avenue, Canmore, Alberta,
Canada T1W 1P6

Copyright 1997, 1999
© Altitude Publishing Canada Ltd.
Text copyright 1997 © Kevin Van Tighem

9 8 7 6

Canadian Cataloguing in Publication Data
Van Tighem, Kevin, 1952 -
Bears

(An Altitude SuperGuide to Nature)
ISBN 1-55153-811-3

1. Bears--Canada, Western. 2. Bears--Northwestern
States. I. Title. II. Series.
QL737.C27V36 1997   599.74'446'09712   C96-
910757-9

Altitude GreenTree Program
Altitude will plant in Canada twice as many trees as
were used in the manufacturing of this product.

Made in Western Canada
Printed and bound in Canada
by Friesen Printers, Altona, Manitoba

Front cover photo: Grizzly Bear

Frontispiece: Close-up of Grizzly Bear

Back cover photo: Grizzly bear

Back cover inset photo: Black bear cubs

Production
Art direction & design	Stephen Hutchings
Project management	Sharon Komori
Layout	Sharon Komori
Editor	Lynn Zwicky
Editorial Assistant	Sabrina Grobler
Index/Proofreading	Elizabeth Bell
Financial management	Laurie Smith
Sales management	Scott Davidson

A Note from the Publisher
The world described in *Altitude SuperGuides* is a
unique and fascinating place. It is a world filled with
surprise and discovery, beauty and enjoyment, questions and answers. It is a world of people, cities, landscape, animals and wilderness as seen through the
eyes of those who live in, work with, and care for this
world. The process of describing this world is also a
means of defining ourselves.

It is also a world of relationship, where people de-
rive their meaning from a deep and abiding contact
with the land—as well as from each other. And it is
this sense of relationship that guides all of us at Altitude to ensure that these places continue to survive
and evolve in the decades ahead.

Altitude SuperGuides are books intended to be
used, as much as read. Like the world they describe,
Altitude SuperGuides are evolving, adapting and
growing. Please write to us with your comments and
observations, and we will do our best to incorporate
your ideas into future editions of these books.

Stephen Hutchings
Publisher

Contents

Acknowledgements

This book owes its existence to the many people who contributed their knowledge, skills and energies to help me pull it together. Bill Dolan, Rob Watt and my other colleagues generously filled in for me during the months that I took off work to write the book. Gail Van Tighem, my wife and favourite field companion, put up with my late nights and random piles of papers long after anyone else would have booted me out to the garage. She also proofread and critiqued the whole text.

Information for this book came from a great variety of sources—both individuals and published materials. Thanks go, in particular, to Arlene Bethune, Ray DeMarchi, Maureen Enns, Keith Everts, Craig Fager, Stephen Herrero, the late Ian Jack, Eric Langshaw, Wayne McCrory, Paul Paquet, Steve Pozzanghera, Andy Russell, Charlie Russell, Doug and Lynn Seus, David Spalding, Beth Russell-Towe, Rob Watt, John Weaver and John Woods, as well as staff of various state and provincial wildlife agencies who responded promptly to information requests.

Wayne McCrory provided a valuable critical review of the entire text and challenged me to improve it in many ways. I also appreciate the comments of those who reviewed portions of the text: Maureen Enns, Peter Jowett, Paul Paquet, Charlie Russell, Beth Russell-Towe and Gail Van Tighem.

To the extent that this book is thorough and accurate, it's in large part due to the generous help of these and others who remain unnamed. On the other hand, any errors that survived the many edits are mine alone.

Lastly, I extend my special appreciation to the bears and wild places of Western Canada. I dedicate this book to them and to my three children: Corey, Katie and Brian.

How to Use this Book

This is more than a book about the bears of western Canada and the Northwestern United States. It's a book about people—people who study wild bears, who live in places where bears still survive and who work to protect or manage them. It's also a book about how people think about bears. You can use this book to develop an in-depth understanding of the featured species, and you can also use this book to explore how we perceive and live with animals that are capable of killing us—and that almost always choose not to.

If you want to learn about bears in general and some of the conservation issues that affect them, chapters 2 and 3 are good places to spend some time.

If specific topics interest you—such as bear safety, hunting of bears, conservation issues or people or places that you come across in the book—check the index. Because of the way we present information in these Altitude *SuperGuides*, you may encounter the same subject, from a different angle, in different places. The index will help you tie the bits together.

Each species of bear that lives in western North America has a chapter of its own. The polar bear chapter is brief since this species more commonly occurs in other regions. These chapters begin with basic biology information—where to find the species, what the species eats, how it breeds and so forth—and concludes with a discussion of conservation issues affecting the species.

If you're interested in going into the wilds and getting to know bears and their habitat personally, you'll find a wealth of useful tips in chapter 8. It shows how seasoned field biologists find bears and read the signs of bear activity.

Finally, pages 152 - 155 list some contacts and addresses for more information about bears or about ways to help promote the conservation and management of the animals you will meet in this Altitude *SuperGuide.*

Foreword

I probably saw my first bear sometime in the early 1960s on a visit with my parents to the old Banff garbage dump. Like many others in those days, we liked to watch black bears scramble about in piles of refuse—it was a highlight of any park visit. As a member of a family of anglers and hunters, and later as a wilderness hiker and biologist, I've been around bears one way or another ever since.

My Bear Beginnings

I thought I knew bears, and was smug in my own comfortable attitude toward them, until the summer of 1983. I worked that year on a wildlife inventory of two rugged mountain parks in British Columbia: Mount Revelstoke and Glacier national parks. A colleague returned early one day from his fieldwork after a black bear had chased him up a tree. I ribbed him about letting a mere black bear cow him and later went out to the site to complete the sampling he'd left unfinished.

In dense aspen forest I paused, suddenly aware of a prickling tension in the air. A large male black bear was watching me, about thirty metres away. No cause for concern. I raised my arms high to make myself look as large as possible, and yelled at him. It had always worked before. But this bear slowly lowered his head, half-turned toward me and fixed me with a cold, hostile gaze.

My legs went rubbery. My cockiness had switched to helpless fear. Death, I realized now, might be seconds away. Even as I looked around for a safe retreat, I knew in the back of my mind that I had behaved like a disrespectful boor, invading the bear's peace and privacy with my loud and aggressive behaviour. Weak with fear, I eased quietly away through the trees. The bear, mercifully, simply watched me go.

A week later, a helicopter dropped me and my wife Gail off on the brushy floodplain of the Incommapleux River for more fieldwork. As we set up camp, I spotted a young grizzly about to cross the river toward us. I shouted and waved my arms to get the bear's attention and, finally, it saw me and retreated back up the hill.

Next morning, I encountered yet another bear. I could hear it moving about uphill in dense avalanche alder, so I shouted and whistled to let it know I was there. No doubt curious about the strange sounds, the bear promptly sneaked closer to investigate. Hearing the faint rustling of twigs, I crouched to look beneath the alders and came face-to-face with a startled grizzly. Within seconds, I was five metres up a lone spruce tree and the bear, no doubt as shocked as me, had vanished.

Next day, yet another grizzly encounter. Gail had headed out by now and the helicopter dropped me high

Grizzly bear in the rough

encounters with bears over too short a time had eroded my easy confidence.

That September, I woke in the dark of an unforgettable night to the ring of the phone. My father's voice was almost unrecognizable. I felt the cold paralysis of fear clamp down on my heart as he struggled to tell me the news. He was calling from a hospital emergency ward: a grizzly had severely mauled my little sister and her husband. They had been hiking and surprised the bear on a sheep carcass in a snow flurry.

This sort of thing isn't easy to write about. Thirteen years later, I still struggle with the sense that somehow it should have been me, not her. Her injuries continue to plague her; their lives have changed forever. Friends and family have suffered with them.

That strange and disconcerting year took me from thinking about bears in a superficial, self-satisfied manner to trying to come to terms with what bears really are, and how we might live with them. I have watched, contemplated, read about and discussed bears many times since then. I have come to know a few bears as individuals; watched others try to coexist with humans only to die at their hands; struggled to break through my own biases and fears to a real understanding of these fascinating, intelligent and potentially dangerous wild animals.

I don't know if I'll ever succeed. This book, in any case, is a product of the effort.

in an alpine basin, alone. No sooner had I picked out a campsite than I noticed movement out of the corner of my eye and spotted a very large grizzly picking his way across the mountain slope above me. Reaching a gully full of old snow, the bear sat down on his haunches and tobogganed down the slope, breaking into a trot at the bottom and emerging into the small meadow where I had left my food and supplies. Not knowing how else to keep him from stumbling on my cache, I shot some pen flares at him. The bear turned and fled down an avalanche path.

I slept poorly that night, alone in my small tent. In the morning, the mist-shrouded mountain slopes looked ominous. Too many chance

Introduction

Bears are bigger than we are—more powerful, more dangerous. They haunt the edges of the forests of our imagination. They grow larger than life as night approaches. Small children lie awake in the dark, listening for bears outside the tent.

Their parents listen too. Out there, bears prowl the shadows. Overhead, the Great Bear stalks out of myth across a sea of stars.

Since the dawn of time, humans and bears have lived uneasily together, sharing the same foods and the same preferred habitats, avoiding one another as much as possible out of wariness and fear.

Almost every aboriginal culture had its bear cult, a secret society reserved for the strongest, most dangerous warriors. Killing a bear has long counted as proof of the highest bravery. Skinned, a bear looks eerily human, adding to its supernatural mystique.

Fear of bears defines part of what it is to be human. Our species emerged out of the depths of time into a world already populated by these great carnivores. Before we mastered iron and, later, invented firearms, we had few defences against them—only watchful caution, and elaborate ceremonies and sacrifices to ward off harm.

Kootenae Appee, a Piikanii war chief who sought to hinder the explorations of David Thompson two hundred years ago, was reported by Thompson to have said: "Before the white men came to us we were weak. Every year the grizzled bears destroyed many of us; our arrows were headed with stone which broke on them..."

Once we developed better weapons, however, fear became a force for extirpation.

England no longer has bears—human fear killed them all long before the Magna Carta. California once had thousands of grizzlies—now, none. No black bears survive in the hills of Kentucky where, legend says, Davey Crocket killed his first at the age of three. Plains grizzlies no longer roam the breaks of the Saskatchewan and Missouri rivers. Polar bears no longer forage along the edges of the lower St. Lawrence River.

Where human populations grow, bears dwindle or disappear. When we return to the wild, to places where bears still survive, all our primeval fears awaken again. The risk of a car accident on the way to bear country far outstrips the risk of a close-range encounter with a bear, but it's the bear that worries us as we hurtle down the pavement at a hundred kilometres an hour.

Why do bears frighten us so? How are we to live with them in a shrinking world?

More to the point, how are they to live with us?

left: A black bear forages for dandelions

The Quality of Mercy

We used to have few defences against bears. Now bears have few defences against us. The sheer weight of human numbers—5.5 billion and counting—and the imperative of human ambitions leave precious little room for other dominant animals in the earth's beleaguered ecosystems.

Biologist Charlie Russell has studied bears at closer range and with greater sympathy than most other people. In his book *Spirit Bear*, Charlie describes many brushes with the large bears of B.C.'s coastal rain forest—bears hunting for food—that passed without any aggressive behaviour on the part of the bears. The bears could have crushed him, but they didn't.

Many people have described encounters at close range with grizzly and black bears that—popular

above: Two grizzly cubs scamper across a clearing in the woods

prejudice tells us—should have led to disaster. Instead, the bears usually fled or paid no attention. At worst, they might have shown a persistent sort of curiosity.

Most bear encounters end peacefully. Bears have far more to fear from a human encounter than humans from a bear encounter—our exaggerated fear adds to the bears' risk.

Maybe we should take a lesson from the quality of mercy in bears, their restraint and reserve. We have arrived at a time in the earth's history when the future of bears and many lesser animals now depends on our ability to demonstrate those same qualities of mercy, restraint and reserve.

If we learn to understand bears better, that will be a start.

Bears in Human Culture

Most First Nations have viewed the bear as a being of great power—potentially a great ally, sometimes a great enemy. Some First Nations hunted bears; others had taboos about killing bears except in self-defence. Many tribes considered killing a bear one of the greatest feats of bravery. A warrior risked his life to do it, especially in the days before firearms and horses, when he faced his adversary—an animal as much as four times his weight—with nothing more than stone-tipped arrows, spears or atlatls.

North America's First Peoples

Tribes along the coasts of what are now British Columbia and Alaska often carved bear images into totems, a place of high esteem.

The Nuu-chah-nulth, who have occupied Canada's west coast for millennia, have long recognized the potent spirituality of the bears that share the coastal forests, salmon streams and salal tangles of their homeland.

George Woodcock, in his book *Peoples of the Coast*, describes the ceremonial honour accorded bears killed for meat and hides. In the Nuu-chah-nulth village of Tahsis, hunters placed a bear they had killed in a sitting position facing the chief. They adorned it with the ceremonial headdress of a chief and dusted the dead guest with eagle's down. They then skinned and butchered the bear and cooked its meat in a stew.

At the feast that followed, only a small number of people ate the bear stew, because anyone who ate bear meat had to abstain from eating salmon for several weeks to avoid offending the fish.

European Attitudes toward Bears

In primitive times, the warrior people of northern Europe viewed bears in much the same way as North American first peoples. They considered the bear alternately a gentle giant and a dangerously powerful and implacable foe, and believed it to be a totemic animal of great power.

Honoring the Dead

When Kwakwa'ka'wakw hunters killed a bear, they honoured the power of the animal with ceremonies before they butchered the carcass. In one ceremony, described by an early anthropologist, the hunter placed his hand against the paw of the fallen bear and recited a short prayer thanking the bear, as a friend, for making the hunt a success. The hunter then asked the bear to share its power of capturing salmon and other game.

left: On a totem pole in Vancouver, the figure of a bear is positioned beneath a Thunderbird

Killing a bear, eating its heart or donning its hide, they believed, could give men bearlike qualities.

Donald Ward writes, in a commentary on a collection of German folklore, that hunting cultures believed that humans turned into animals when they wore animal skins. They also believed that "predators (bears, wolves, tigers...) have essentially human cores. It is thought that should they choose to walk around as humans, they would only need to shed their animal skins." These ancient beliefs, he says, evolved into the idea of were-animals.

Certain great warriors were famous for working themselves into frenzies in battle, convinced that they had the strength and power of bears. The Vikings and some of the northern German tribes called such warriors *berserkers*, from *ber* (bear) and *serkr* (hide). The English word "berserk" comes from the same root.

J.R.R. Tolkien, a British professor who studied ancient European languages, drew the plot of his famous fantasy novel, *The Hobbit*, from the mythologies and folktales of Europe. He based one of his characters, Beorn, on the berserker tradition.

Bears of the Star Fields

The Big Dipper, one of the first constellations children learn to identify, forms part of a larger constellation called *Ursa Major*, which means "great bear" in Latin.

Ursa Major gets its name from a Greek myth about Zeus and one of his many infidelities. Zeus was married to Hera, but fell in love with Callisto. When Hera learned of the affair she swore vengeance, so Zeus turned Callisto into a bear to disguise her from his furious wife.

Looking like a bear, however, carried its own risks. One day Callisto's son, Arcas, saw a bear—really his mother—and raised his spear to kill it. To protect Callisto, Zeus quickly changed Arcas into a bear cub. Then, to head off future disasters, he put both bears among the stars. Hera saw this and finally got her revenge. She decreed that both bears would never rest again and doomed them to rotate endlessly in the night sky.

Finnish tradition says the bear lives in the sky with his family—the stars in the Big Dipper are Otava and his brothers.

The Big Dipper also has associations with bears in the mythologies of many of North America's first peoples. The Kainai have a story of a young woman caught mating with a bear in the forest. Her brothers killed the bear, leaving their sister to mourn her lost lover. She cut off his paws to remember him by and returned to her home. There she faced taunting and humiliation. Finally, someone so angered her that she roared—she had become a bear.

When the brothers discovered what happened, they fled. Their sister pursued them, in spite of the powers of one brother who put obstacles in her way. Eventually she caught up with them and treed them.

The bear-woman began to shake her brothers from the tree, but the

Tolkien writes "...you must be careful not to annoy him, or heaven knows what will happen. He can be appalling when he is angry, though he is kind enough if humoured. Still, I warn you he gets angry easily...He is a skin-changer. He changes his skin; sometimes he is a huge black bear, sometimes he is a great strong black-haired man with huge arms and a great beard."

The nations civilized under the Roman Empire, however, did not revere bears. They were obsessed with imposing human order and control on nature, and saw bears as a symbol of nature's power and savagery. These cultures tortured bears to death, perhaps to demonstrate man's triumph over nature's fury.

Histories say the Roman emperor Gordian liked to watch bloody matches between bears and dogs or gladiators, and witnessed the death of close to a thousand bears. England's Queen Elizabeth I reportedly enjoyed the sight of 13 bears being torn apart by dogs.

Europeans also trained bears as clowns. The act of reducing a wild carnivore to a silly-looking entertainer bore the same symbolism as

Bears of the Star Fields

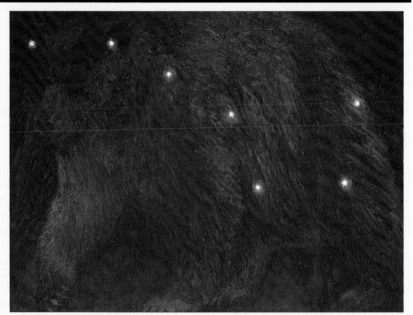

Ursa Major *as depicted in a painting by Dan Hudson*

powerful brother shot her with an arrow. She fell, dead, and turned back into their sister. When the brothers saw their sister lying dead, they felt so remorseful that they agreed to go somewhere far away and never return. The powerful brother then shot an arrow into the sky and they followed it. They became the Seven Brothers— the seven stars of the Big Dipper.

bearbaiting. It was less lethal, but just as destructive of wild bears.

When Europeans arrived in the New World, they brought their ambivalent view of bears with them, an ambivalence that North America's abundant black bears reinforced. Europeans viewed these bears—curious, occasionally entertaining, sometimes destructive—as lovable clowns at times, and, at other times, as dangerous marauders.

Bears in Modern Culture

Bears are everywhere and nowhere in modern culture.

At a time in history when the vast majority of North Americans have never seen a real bear, bears of human conception abound in books, art, movies, the names of sports teams and countless consumer products. Children grow up hugging teddy bears, listening to Winnie-the-Pooh stories and enjoying Yogi Bear cartoons on morning television. Teenagers watch movies such as *Grizzly* ("18 feet of gut-crunching terror!"). Conservation groups auction paintings of bears to raise money.

We call them "bears," but really these images amount to little more than furry reflections of human fears, wishes and fond imaginings. Few come close to representing the real living creatures. Few try.

North American culture has three popular images of bears: lovable clown, marauding monster and besieged wilderness creature.

The lovable clown appears in Walt Disney movies, Yogi and Booboo cartoons, Winnie-the-Pooh, Paddington stories and other children's literature. This image fits with the early days of North American tourism when parks and resorts used feeding programs or strategically placed garbage dumps to lure in bears for the entertainment of middle-class tourists. The bears were amusing at first—standing on their hind legs and waddling awkwardly to reach food, getting into flour or molasses, and emerging smeared and clownlike.

Inevitably, this treatment spoiled many bears. They became aggressive and had to be killed to protect tourists. The "marauding monster" image of bears probably comes from this, reinforced by the frontier myth of the killer grizzly.

"At the turn of the century and for the next thirty or forty years, we saw

Shape Shifters

Finns and Laplanders had many stories about werebears and a few about werewolves. Many stories tell of a woman married to a man who sometimes took the shape of a bear. One evening when the man knew he would soon become a bear, he grew worried for her safety and told her he would have to leave her for a while. He warned her to watch out for a bear. Sure enough, that night, a huge bear attacked her, but she was ready and escaped to safety. Later she learned the truth about the bear. Once she knew the truth, her husband was freed of his curse.

the animal as a dangerous part of the landscape," says wildlife artist Maureen Enns. "We always saw the bear with claws extended, mouth open."

That image appears often in the work of Frederick Remington, Charlie Russell and other frontier painters, and in Ernest Thompson Seton's book *Biography of a Grizzly*. It continues to show up far too often in taxidermy. It comes from the fears and insecurities of men confronted by wilderness, a landscape they did not understand and that magnified their sense of mortality. In the mythology of the old West, all rivers were torrents, all grizzlies man-eaters and all native people savages.

Today, the marauding bear survives mostly in horror stories and B-movies such as *Grizzly*, where a giant rampaging grizzly bear fights helicopters and eats attractive women.

James Oliver Curwood's classic frontier novel, *The Grizzly King*, was the basis for the early 1990s movie *The Bear*. The movie starred a trained Kodiak bear named Bart as a grizzly who adopts an orphaned cub and fights to protect him from a guide and a hunter who invade their wilderness refuge. The book and the movie represent another image of bears, one increasingly common as the twentieth century has unfolded: the bear as fascinating but beleaguered wilderness creature. In the realm of nonfiction, Andy Russell's *Grizzly Country* captures a powerful version of this image.

But in serving as icons for human superiority over lesser creatures (the friendly clown image), our ability to control nature (the marauding monster bear) or our nostalgia for paradise lost (beleaguered wilderness creature), the bears that populate modern North American culture have little in common with the real animal.

Maureen Enns discovered this in the course of a three-year project to paint, film and write about the grizzlies of Banff National Park as "monarchs of the wilderness." She started from the premise that grizzly bears symbolize North America's dwindling

Bears are commonly represented in totem poles

wilderness—creatures fleeing from or fighting against the incursions of modern man. As she spent more time in bear country, however, she found herself seeing a very different animal than the one she thought she already knew.

Her experience has led her to a new kind of bear art that looks for the bear where it really lives, rather than among the popular prejudices of a society that has become, as one naturalist once said, "orphaned from nature."

Tourism and Bears

Bears are fascinating animals and most live in beautiful natural areas. It should come as no surprise, then, that the interests of bears and the tourism industry overlap. Too often, the bears come out the losers. A growing number of tourism operators, however,

Bart

Movie stars that weigh more than 600 kilograms (1,400 pounds) don't normally get starring roles. Bart, however, is an exception. He is a huge Kodiak bear, one of several animals that Doug and Lynn Seus have trained for movie roles at their large compound in Heber Valley, Utah. Bart has appeared in such movies as *The Bear, Legends of the Fall, Clan of the Cave Bear*, and Disney's *White Fang*. More recently, in his honorary affiliation with *Vital Ground*, a conservation organization dedicated to protecting privately owned grizzly bear habitat, Bart has become a living ambassador for his beleaguered wild relatives.

Teddy bears originated when the popular American president Theodore Roosevelt made headlines in 1902 by refusing to kill a black bear. His hunting companions, concerned that the president hadn't had much luck, ran a black bear down with hounds. After a fierce struggle during which the bear killed one of the dogs, they chained the bear to a tree for Roosevelt to shoot. Roosevelt, an ardent conservationist who believed strongly in the principles of fair chase, indignantly refused to kill the helpless animal.

The Washington Post commemorated the president's action in a cartoon that quickly became famous as an icon for sportsmanlike restraint. It caught the attention of Morris Michtom, a Brooklyn entrepreneur. Michtom's wife had designed a toy bear, so Michtom wrote the president and asked permission to market the toy as "Teddy's Bear."

Roosevelt wrote back, "I don't think my name will mean much to the bear business, but you're welcome to use it."

He was wrong. Teddy's Bears caught on and their range expanded rapidly into the homes of virtually every small child in North America.

Roosevelt later became one of the founders of the Boone and Crockett Society, an organization that promotes sportsmanship and fair chase in hunting.

Teddy Bears

want to turn tourism into a force for bear conservation.

Banff National Park exemplifies a serious conflict between bears and conventional tourism. The federal government established the park in 1885 as a scenic tourist destination to help pay off the immense debt of Canada's coast-to-coast railroad. The park now has more development than any other national park in North America. A four-lane express-way slices through the Bow Valley, once one of the most productive bear habitats in the park. Resort hotels, golf courses and towns sprawl out from the highway, eliminating habitat, blocking important wildlife corridors and filling the landscape with bear-curious, but bear-ignorant tourists. Remote parts of Banff National Park still shelter important wilderness terrain, but bears can hardly use the critically important

The Genealogy of Pooh

Arthur A. Milne was a novelist, playwright and essayist who wrote frequently for the prestigious London-based magazine *Punch*. Milne was educated at Cambridge and was a friend of H.G. Wells.

He modelled the character of Christopher Robin on his own son, Christopher, who received his now-famous teddy bear from his parents for his first birthday on August 21, 1921. Milne based Winnie-the-Pooh on the toy bear and on a real one—young Christopher and his father frequently visited the real Winnie at the London Zoo.

Winnie-the-Pooh was born not in England, but somewhere near White River, Ontario. A young army officer named Harry Colebourn got off the train there in late August, 1914, and met a hunter who had killed a black bear and captured her small female cub. Colebourn, a veterinarian by training, bought the cub and took it with him when, soon after, he shipped overseas to England with the 2nd Canadian Infantry Brigade.

Colebourn named the little bear Winnie after Winnipeg, his hometown. Winnie soon became a familiar sight around camp, trailing after Colebourn and other soldiers and begging for food. The brigade adopted her as its mascot. When the soldiers shipped out for France in December, Colebourn had to make arrangements for the little bear's care. He lent her to the London Zoo where he visited her often during his leaves. He formally donated her to the zoo in 1918.

Winnie became a popular attraction at the zoo, entertaining thousands of British children before she died at the ripe old age of 30.

The famous drawings of Pooh, however, depict a third bear: a toy belonging to Graham Sheppard, son of illustrator E.H. Sheppard. Sheppard, whom *Punch* hired in 1921, was one of the first illustrators to receive a share of book royalties. Milne insisted on giving Sheppard 20 per cent, in recognition of the role his drawings played in the success of Milne's books.

Sheppard also illustrated Kenneth Grahame's *The Wind in the Willows*.

montane habitats of the Bow River valley anymore.

"Banff," says Harvey Locke, past-president of the Canadian Parks and Wilderness Society, "is a national disgrace."

Tourism development inside national parks, though excessive, does follow some rules. Banff, for example, requires all businesses to use a bear-proof garbage system and has begun working with tourism operators to educate tourists about responsible behaviour in bear country. Even so, Mike McIvor—a longtime Banff resident and critic of Parks Canada's failure to put the brakes on runaway development—says parks officials downplay scientific evidence and public concern about the impact of commercial tourism on bears and other wildlife.

Banff's problems have deep roots. Canada had a well-established tourism industry long before biologists knew much about bear ecology and the importance of healthy, natural landscapes. Besides, when the early hotels went up, wild country and bears seemed inexhaustible. No longer. In 1996, a task force commissioned by Canada's Minister of Environment concluded that the only way to save Banff's bears is to actually remove some hotels and other developments, and put quotas on hiking trails.

Other projects threaten bear habitat nearby. West of Invermere, in B.C., investors want to develop a massive downhill ski resort around the Jumbo Glacier in the heart of some of the best grizzly bear habitat in the Purcell Mountains.

Kananaskis Country, east of Banff, faces a flood of development proposals. In southwestern Alberta, a resort expansion in the West Castle Valley threatens to block a vitally important grizzly and black bear movement corridor that connects Alberta's bear populations with those of southeastern B.C and northern Montana.

The demand for weekend homes—another form of tourism—also takes a bite out of bear habitat, adding to the recreational pressure nibbling away at the wilderness. Each new cabin, summer home or acreage may prove a problem source of garbage or food, or create another locus of human activity that bears avoid.

Ecotourism offers the intriguing possibility that tourism may become a force for the conservation, rather than the destruction, of North America's bears. Ecotourism shuns resorts and other man-made attractions. It considers healthy wildlife populations and unspoiled natural habitats the most valuable capital assets for Western Canada's tourism industry. Ecotourism operators offer high-quality, nature-based experiences with skilled guides, rather than luxury accommodation and convention facilities in the heart of what was once wild nature. Rather than seeing wilderness protection as an obstacle to tourism, ecotourism businesses see it as critical to their industry's success.

In the late 1980s and early 1990s, commercial wildlife-viewing tour operators and whitewater rafting companies played a major role in building public demand for protected

continued on page 28

Andy Russell's *Grizzly Country*

Andy Russell was four years old in 1919 when his family moved to the spectacular aspen parkland country that sprawls along the foot of the Rocky Mountains, south of Pincher Creek.

Andy grew up exploring the canyons and headwaters of the Rocky Mountain front ranges, hunting big game, fishing and running into the occasional grizzly bear. Those explorations served him well when, in 1936, he went to work for legendary outfitter Bert Riggall.

In 1937, Andy married Bert Riggall's oldest daughter, Kay, and a few years later took over the outfitting business. For several years Kay and Andy continued to guide hunters, fishermen and adventurers into the wilderness country of the upper Oldman, Castle and Flathead rivers.

But wilderness had little value for mid-twentieth century society. As industry and the Alberta government pushed roads into the backcountry for oil, coal and timber, Andy found it harder and harder to offer clients the solitude, untrammelled countryside and abundant wildlife that his father-in-law had taken for granted. Even Waterton Lakes National Park, though free of industrial development, was becoming too tame and regulated as its popularity with tourists grew.

In 1960, Andy Russell closed down the outfitting business Bert Riggall had started half a century earlier.

"I knew that outfitting was finished, at least the way I'd known it," he says. "At the time, we were one of the top

Andy Russell

three outfits on the continent, but I'd seen what happened to some of these other guys who tried to hang on after it was too late, and I decided it was time to change careers."

Andy became a wildlife cinematographer and conservation educator. He contracted for two short wildlife films and then, with his oldest boys Dick and Charlie, embarked on a major project to film grizzlies in the shrinking wildernesses of Waterton Lakes National Park, B.C.'s Flathead Valley and the remote mountains of northern Alaska.

The resulting movie, *Grizzly Country*, presents a remarkable chronicle of an animal that depends, like Andy himself, on an undervalued and fast-vanishing heritage—wilderness. The Russells made the entire film without even the protection of a rifle, working at close range with bears considered the deadliest predators in North America. Learning as they went

Andy Russell's *Grizzly Country*

Grizzly country

about the tolerant side of the great bears, Andy and his sons began to revolutionize the common wisdom that all bears are dangerous.

Andy toured North America for 11 years with the film, showing its unequalled footage to audiences in Boston, New York, Toronto and dozens of other cities.

"That was a tough way to make a living—living out of a suitcase, having to deal with different strangers all the time," he recalls.

But everywhere he went, his movie played to packed houses, often to standing-room-only crowds. Andy held them spellbound with his down-to-earth narration, a skill honed around countless flickering campfires. People saw grizzly bears portrayed as never before—as real animals rather than savage killers.

Movies cost a lot to produce, so Andy decided to write a book to help finance his film. He flew to New York

and had lunch with the editor-in-chief of Alfred A. Knopf Publishing.

"I showed him a selection of a hundred or so wildlife photographs I'd brought out with me," says Andy, "There were pictures of the head and shoulders of a grizzly, all kinds of wildlife photos. He just looked at them for a while, and then he said, 'Andy how the hell did you manage to get pictures like this?'

"I said, 'That's what I'm here for: I want to write you a book that will tell exactly how I got those pictures.'"

Grizzly Country, the book, was published in 1967 and became an instant best-seller. More than 100,000 copies have sold so far around the world. *Grizzly Country*'s anecdotal style and in-depth, sympathetic portrayal of grizzlies and the threats to their wilderness habitat have played a pivotal role in building public awareness of the value and vulnerability of bears and other wildlife.

Today, a small but growing movement seeks to restore some of the wilderness where Andy filmed Grizzly Country thirty years ago. Locally based conservation organizations such as the Friends of the Flathead and the Castle-Crown Wilderness Coalition are lobbying the Alberta and B.C. governments to close roads and restore wild habitat southwest of Pincher Creek and in the upper Flathead River basin.

Their efforts build on the public concern spawned by the work of pioneer conservationists such as Andy Russell.

Maureen Enns'Grizzly Kingdom

I was in Africa doing an art project on the African elephant...and I started thinking that I'd spent the last five years working on other continents dealing with animals not directly related to Canadian conservation and why wasn't I working in Canada? And my answer was that I was afraid to work in Canada—it's easier if you do something in another country and get out. The fallout isn't as great.

So I decided I couldn't shirk this any more, that I wanted to say something about the Canadian wilderness. I've lived in the eastern slopes of the Rocky Mountains for about eighteen years and I thought, "Well it's under fire just like everywhere else in the world." I thought of the grizzly as monarch of the mountains, the animal that represented the wildest of the wild country.

When I first talked to Banff National Park, I wanted to do an art project and a documentary about the monarch of the Canadian Rockies...I would say wonderful things about our wilderness and there was...not going to be any fallout politically, which of course proved not to be possible.

In that first year I had one amazing encounter with a mother and her two cubs. In the second year, I started to find more bears and more amazing things happened. My focus started to shift: I was no longer just looking at the grizzly and its mountain habitat, the relationship between "monarch" and "wilderness." Here was an animal that wasn't performing according to everything I'd read and understood, and

questions emerged in my mind: "What's going on here? Have I been fed a whole bunch of information in my life that isn't true?"

I was making a few notes to that effect in some of the cabin journals in the park. It didn't take too long before the word was out that I was absolutely out to lunch about bears and that my whole project should be shut down.

When the book finally came out, the park wardens almost died. I'd met [bear researcher] Charlie Russell in the process of all this because, as I kept questioning why bears weren't acting fearful or aggressive, someone suggested I call up Charlie Russell. I did, and I think I blew all the circuits in my brain in one phone conversation. I was learning astonishing things about bears. I went down and interviewed Charlie. He invited me to Princess Royal Island in B.C. and, sure enough, Princess Royal Island and Charlie's experiences confirmed everything I had suspected about bears and it's just gone on from there.

I think we have never really looked at the reality of the bear ...we have tunnel vision in our culture. We're told: "This is how things are, this is the way you behave, this is what you do." And we don't question it.

I sort of grew up with certain expectations about grizzlies: if they're in the area, then you immediately leave because they're going to cause trouble; if your horse gets near one, it'll probably rear up and buck you off; and if you get between a mother and her cubs or a bear and its kill, they'll

Maureen Enns'Grizzly Kingdom

Maureen Enns and her painting, Queen of the Rockies.

and her cub came walking right toward us but my cameraman bolted so I didn't get a chance to really play that one out. What I found curious was how calm she stayed.

Later that summer, I was riding down the Cascade fire road and there was a female and cub right beside the road. The horses spotted her. They weren't upset at all, so I just stopped the horses and sat there, and the horses actually started to go to sleep! They propped up their feet and started to doze off. The mother and cub were just foraging on the grasses, and the cub looked as if she wanted to come over and look at the horses. I thought, "I don't want this cub under their feet" so I got the horse to back up a little bit and the cub seemed to get the message. This went on for about twenty minutes. They were maybe twenty feet away.

I haven't finished. I thought I would be finished with this. This is the first time one project has carried on into another project, but I feel like I'm not even halfway there in understanding the bear and what it really is…

charge instantly—and that is by and large true about a kill, you can't expect any different behaviour on that one.

Well, once during the first year I rode over this little knoll and surprised some little grizzly cubs about thirty feet away. I couldn't see the mother. Then I spotted her, and she was just covered with blood! She'd just killed an elk. And I was sitting on a horse!

But my horse didn't seem all that upset.

The mother just sort of looked at us and moseyed around. Her cubs scampered over to her and she just wandered away and nothing happened. I think it would have been different if I had been on foot, but it told me that everything doesn't always happen the way I expected.

In the second year, another mother

wilderness in B.C. The immense Tatsenshini River watershed—threatened with copper mining—got protection as a wilderness preserve after commercial rafting operators took journalists, politicians and other influential people on wilderness excursions down the river. Similarly, ecotourism operators helped argue, successfully, that the Khutzeymateen watershed near Prince Rupert had more value to the province of B.C. as a bear sanctuary than as another logged-out valley.

Beth Russell-Towe, who owns an art and souvenir shop in Waterton Lakes National Park, has spearheaded a visionary way to link tourism to bear conservation. She worries about the rate of habitat fragmentation around the great national parks in the U.S. and Canadian Rockies. She knows that if parks become isolated islands of wilderness, their bear populations will become increasingly vulnerable to extinction. Their great bears gone, the parks would lose not just their ecological wholeness, but their souls.

In the mid-1980s, Russell-Towe coined a tourism-marketing idea now internationally known as the "Trail of the Great Bear." The trail comprises a network of scenic travel routes that connect Yellowstone National Park—the first national park in the U.S.A. and home of the southernmost surviving population of North American grizzlies—with Waterton-Glacier International Peace Park, and then with Banff National Park—Canada's first—and Jasper National Park. By drawing a

Beth Russell-Towe: Tourism for Bears

I was born in the American mid-west, but I've lived in the Rockies for more than 25 years now. Back in 1985, several of us helped set up the UNESCO biosphere reserve around Waterton Lakes National Park. A whole lot of things were happening at the same time—the Canadian national parks' centennial, a developer planning a huge waterslide park right on the Waterton boundary. We all started to realize that we really needed to come out with strong advocacy for parks and protected areas.

Archaeologist Barney Reeves, bear researcher Chuck Jonkel and I were the core group in developing the Trail of the Great Bear. There was a lot of money available in government-grant programs during those early years and we made a lot of progress. Now we're having to look at longer time-lines and more modest expectations in the new financial realities, but we're making progress all the time.

I see the great bear very much as a symbol of wilderness and the integrity of natural ecosystems.

Beth Russell-Towe, president and founder of the Trail of the Great Bear Society.

Trail of the Great Bear

Box 142, Waterton Park,
Alberta, Canada T0K 2M0
1-800-215-2395

link between the entire tourism corridor and grizzly bear habitat, Russell-Towe and others in the tourism industry hope to give both tourists and business people a stake in conserving bear habitat in the entire region, not just the parks. At the same time, tourists from around the world, as they travel the Trail of the Great Bear through some of the most spectacular surviving bear country in the Rocky Mountains, find more and better opportunities to learn about grizzly bears and their habitat.

Great Links to Ecotourism

http://www.gorp.com/gorp/activity/wildlife.htm

Grizzly Discovery Centre

When a poacher killed their mother, two grizzly bear cubs near Revelstoke, B.C. faced a nearly hopeless future. Rather than leave the young cubs to die, wildlife officers arranged to ship them south to a new home near the border of Yellowstone National Park. Today, the cubs share their new quarters with five other grizzlies, including one from Alaska's Denali National Park and another from Katmai.

The bears live in large outdoor enclosures at the Grizzly Discovery Centre, a facility that opened in the early 1990s amid a cloud of controversy. The Discovery Centre's founders argued that visitors to neighbouring Yellowstone rarely see grizzlies and would benefit from the chance to watch them in a safe setting. They said wild grizzlies would benefit too, since tourists would leave with a better understanding of bears.

Conservation groups and biologists, however, fought the centre down to the wire. They worried that bears might escape the enclosure and expose Yellowstone's vulnerable wild grizzlies to genetic contamination from cross-breeding or, worse, to new diseases. They said wild bears attracted to the centre during breeding season could end up dying as problem bears.

Critics also argued that people satisfied with seeing captive bears would not care about protecting habitat for wild bears.

Today, in the middle of summer, more than a thousand people a day pass through the gates of the Grizzly Discovery Centre. Curator Travis Vineyard says that four years after opening, "We've proven what we set out to do and I think most of the detractors have had their fears allayed."

Emily Williams of the Great Bear Foundation, however, disagrees. "I see it as a roadside attraction charging big bucks for an IMAX and animals in cages that you could see in the wild two miles down the road."

Vineyard says the centre, through its affiliated International Grizzly Fund, works with other groups to put educational kits about bears into schools. It also hires student interns who educate tourists about how to coexist safely with wild bears.

Real Bears

The earliest bears appear in the fossil record of the Miocene geological epoch, about twenty million years ago. They've been around a lot longer than humans. Bears appear to have descended from miacids, a long-extinct line of little tree-climbing creatures that also evolved into dogs and seals. Coincidentally, an early creation myth of the Tahltan people of B.C.'s Stikine Plateau describes a common origin for seals and bears. According to the myth, an immense flood threatened the first people—those who fled into the forest became bears, those who ended up in the water became seals.

Bears in Prehistory

The earliest bearlike animals evolved along three different evolutionary lines. Two lines died out long ago and the third, which first appeared about three million years ago, evolved into all eight modern bear species.

The earliest ancestors of grizzly, black and cave bears all originated 2.5 million years ago in Asia. The cave bear—almost twice the size of our modern grizzly—was extinct by the time the ancestors of the North American black bear ventured east, more than a million years ago, across the land bridge that joined Siberia to Alaska.

Compared to the black bear, grizzlies were latecomers. They arrived in Alaska toward the end of the last Ice Age and spread south across North America only after the continental ice sheets had receded, some twelve to fifteen thousand years ago. Some biologists believe that grizzly bears had not finished spreading east when they encountered Europeans spreading west with guns and strychnine.

This marked the end of range expansion for the grizzly and the beginning of a retreat that continues today.

What Are Bears?

Bears belong to the order *Carnivora*, along with dogs, cats, weasels and raccoons. All carnivores have sharp, elongated canine teeth for puncturing and tearing flesh and molars designed for slicing and shredding.

But black and grizzly bears—the two common bear species of western North America—only occasionally dine on meat, unlike most other carnivores. They are opportunistic omnivores, eating vegetable matter most of the time but taking advantage, when they can, of temporary abundances of fish, insects or meat. Black bears and grizzlies have special adaptations for this un-carnivorous diet: an elongated gut that enables them to extract more food value from vegetable matter than other carnivores—though still far less than deer, elk and other ruminants—and front molars adapted for

left: A black bear in her mountain landscape

continued on page 36

Bears of the World

Only eight species of bears exist in the world, and the International Union for the Conservation of Nature has listed all but the black bear as at risk of extinction. It lists some species as endangered, some as threatened and some as vulnerable. Black, grizzly and polar bears inhabit North America and form the focus of this book. The remaining five species include:

Giant Panda
Fewer than 500 pandas may survive in the wild, making the panda the most endangered of all bear species. Pandas are unique in many ways. Their eyes have slitlike vertical pupils similar to foxes and cats, which probably accounts for the panda's Chinese name that translates as "giant cat-bear." Pandas depend on bamboo forests both for shelter and food. China's growing human population is replacing these forests with agricultural fields. The panda is the symbol of the World Wildlife Fund.

Asiatic Black Bear
This species probably shares an evolutionary ancestor with our North American black bear. It ranges from Pakistan and Afghanistan east to the Pacific Ocean. The demand for bear gallbladders in Chinese and Korean markets has decimated many populations in recent years. Farmers also frequently kill Asian black bears as agricultural pests because they strip bark from trees to get at the sapwood underneath.

Sloth Bear
Sloth bears live in the forests of south-ern Asia and take their name, in part, from the females' habit of carrying cubs on their backs, just like sloths. Fewer than 10,000 survive in the wild because multinational forest companies continue to clearcut the sloth bears' forest habitats. Sloth bears eat ants, termites and honey in addition to vegetation and carrion.

Sun Bear
The sun bear is the smallest bear species in the world, barely half the size of our black bear. Most look disarmingly like black bear cubs, but sun bears occasionally attack humans. Dependent on lowland tropical forests in southeastern Asia, sun bears face multiple threats: deforestation, which destroys their habitat; the gallbladder trade; and coconut plantations, where owners shoot the little bears to protect their trees. Biologists worry that the sun bear may become extinct before scientists have documented even basic biological information about them.

Spectacled Bear
The spectacled bear, the only bear species in South America, appears to have evolved from a giant, long-legged bear that once ranged throughout the western hemisphere. Fewer than 2,000 survive in the wild. Growing populations of slash-and-burn farmers—displaced from fertile lowlands in part by large companies that grow coffee, bananas and other luxury crops for export—are gradually destroying the cloud forest habitat on which these bears depend.

Is That a Grizzly or a Black Bear?

It isn't always easy to tell bears apart. Many people, seeing a brown-coloured bear, assume they have spotted a grizzly, but colour doesn't reliably distinguish black bears and grizzlies.

The name "grizzly" comes from the grizzled appearance of many grizzlies, which results from silver-tipped guard hairs protruding from a darker coat. But not all grizzlies are grizzled. Grizzly bears range in colour from whitish to nearly black. Those in the Rocky Mountains are often silver-tipped, but coastal ones tend to be brown. Black bears, in turn, can be black, brown, honey-coloured, or even white.

Size doesn't always help either, since large black bears can be twice the size of small grizzlies. Habitat provides a useful clue—grizzlies are more of an open-country species—but both species overlap extensively.

So how do you know what you're looking at? The important distinguishing features lie in the shape and proportion of the bear's body.

Grizzly:
- Smaller-looking, rounder ears.
- Snout protrudes from "dish-shaped" face.
- Ruff of coarse hair beneath chin.
- Grizzlies have a pronounced hump at shoulders. Adults generally seem higher at the shoulders than the rump.
- Long, often pale-coloured claws.

Black bear:
- Larger, more elongated ears.
- Snout and forehead tend to run together in a straight line.
- Smooth throat.
- Little or no hump. Appears higher at rear end than shoulders.
- Dark claws, rarely noticeable.

How Big is a Bear?

	Weight	Length
Polar bear	300-550 kg (660-1200 lbs)	1.5-3.0 m (6-11 ft)
Grizzly	130-400 kg (280-900 lbs)	1.8-2.5 m (5.5-7.5 ft)
Black bear	90-150 kg (200-325 lbs)	1.2-1.9 m (3.7-6.0 ft)

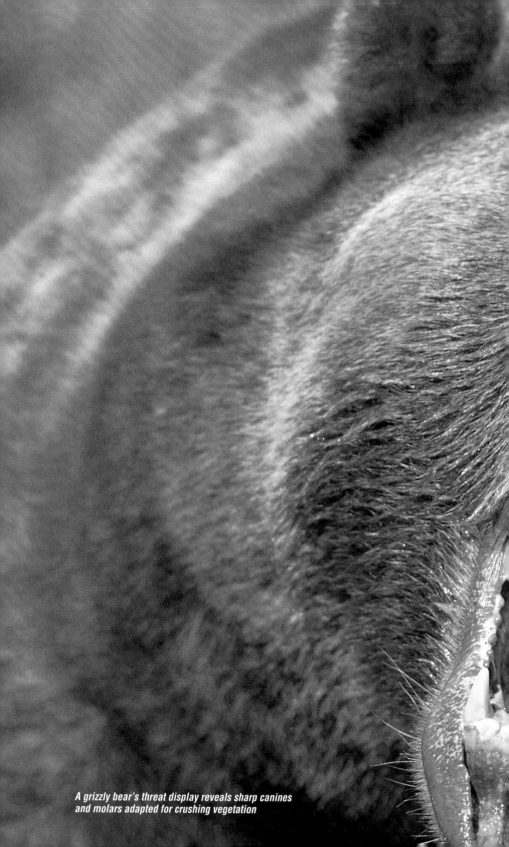

A grizzly bear's threat display reveals sharp canines
and molars adapted for crushing vegetation

crushing rather than slicing.

The flat-footed walk of bears also sets them apart from other carnivores. Bears lay their entire sole and all five toes down with each step. The elongated soles of their hind feet make their tracks resemble human footprints. Their characteristic gait is a shuffling walk, but bears can trot and run, and even walk on their hind legs for a short distance. A bear in a hurry can run twice as fast as a human.

Hibernation

Bears sleep through the winter, unlike wolves, foxes, cougars and other carnivores, which continue to hunt and travel about. Black bears often dig a den under the roots of a tree or, in the temperate rain forests of B.C. and the Pacific Northwest, curl up inside a hollow old cedar tree. Grizzlies that range the Rockies usually excavate dens in the high mountains, where heavy winter snows insulate them. In the old-growth forests of the coastal rain forests, grizzlies, too, use hollow trees.

Many hibernators such as ground squirrels become icy-cold, their body temperatures dropping close to freezing. From time to time, the little animals may wake up briefly to eat, urinate or defecate. The rest of the time, they stay so deeply unconscious that nothing stirs their slumbers.

A bear does not interrupt its hibernation to eat or urinate, so in some ways it sleeps more profoundly than a hibernating rodent. Bears lose body moisture through breathing and evaporation, but they replace it by burning stored fat. In the absence of urination, this would eventually poison the bear—a condition known as uremia—if bears didn't have a unique way to convert urea, and other toxic by-products of metabolism, into protein.

In some ways, though, bears hibernate less deeply than rodents. They remain warm and rouse easily—body temperature only drops seven or eight degrees centigrade, and heartbeat and breathing slow to about half of normal. To maintain themselves during hibernation, bears burn a lot of stored-up fat, up to 4,000 calories a day. Bear fat is exceptionally rich in energy, yielding more than 7,500 calories a kilogram (3,400 calories a pound). An adult male grizzly can curl up for his winter nap with as much as 2.5 million calories of energy stored in rolls beneath his grizzled hide.

Hunger

You won't find many fat vegetarians at the salad bar. That, for a bear, is the whole problem. The need to accumulate a copious supply of fat before winter forces bears to concentrate intently on finding energy-rich

Hungry as a Bear!

A bear can consume up to 20,000 calories of food energy a day. Don Middleton compares this to a human eating 40 hamburgers and 40 sundaes over the course of 24 hours. Researchers in the Yukon found, through analysis of bear droppings, that grizzlies ate as many as a 100,000 buffaloberries a day!

Black bear munching dandelions

food. Any bear that goes to bed in poor condition will likely die before spring.

Meat tops the list of high-quality food. Most bears rely on chance carrion. Some become very effective predators on newborn elk, moose, deer or caribou. Others live in areas where salmon, suckers or other fish spawn in large numbers for part of each year.

Bears spend most of their time, however, feeding on vegetation, insects and other food sources more reliable, if less energy-rich, than meat. Most bears continue to lose weight through early spring, but as their foods come into season, bears may gain more than a kilogram (2.2 pounds) a day.

Bears eat a lot to compensate for the low food energy of their mostly vegetarian diet. Their digestive systems efficiently extract starches, proteins and other easily digested components of foods, and they excrete the rest undigested. Bear scats consequently give useful clues to a bear's diet, since they contain still-recognizable ants, green plants and berries.

The best foods for bears vary with

What Do Bears Eat?				
	Percentage of Diet			
	Meat	**Fish**	**Vegetation**	**Insects**
Polar bear	95	5	0	0
Grizzly	10	5*	80	5
Black bear	15	<1*	75	10
*considerably higher in coastal drainages where salmon and other fish concentrate to spawn				

habitat and season. A plant that is highly nutritious in spring may have little food value later in the summer. Berries are only available in certain habitats late in the summer.

Junk Food

When a bear catches wind of human garbage, barbecues or poorly stored food, it will probably find the temptation irresistible. Bears are compelled to seek out concentrations of food. They can't turn their backs on something their nose tells them will yield a lot of body fat for little effort.

A black bear rummages through garbage at an open dump site

From their earliest beginnings until the 1970s, most national parks had open garbage dumps. They also had small garbage cans distributed in all their high-use areas. Of course, black and grizzly bears discovered these food sources. Their compulsion to accumulate energy overpowers their natural tendency to avoid humans. Park wardens grew to dread each year's predictable cycle of bears becoming more and more comfortable around humans, then becoming aggressive, and finally having to be killed to protect park visitors. According to biologist Wayne McCrory, park wardens in B.C.'s Glacier National Park had orders to shoot grizzly bears on sight. I can recall seeing a notice posted in the Jasper National Park warden office in the late 1970s authorizing wardens to kill black bears on sight in and around the townsite.

Some heavily used campgrounds worked like ecological vacuum cleaners, attracting bears to their inevitable deaths from the whole

Only You Can Prevent Bear Deaths

Every person who contributes to habituating bears by feeding them, by leaving garbage at campsites or along roads, by not handling food properly, by not taking care of fruit trees, pet foods, barbecues or other attractants around the home or farm, is responsible for the loss of bears.
B.C. Ministry of Environment, 1995: Conservation of Grizzly Bears in B.C.

Why Not Just Move the Bears?

Midnight. A few campfires still flicker here and there but the campground is still and quiet. The night is growing cold; cicadas have ceased their trilling and dew has begun to condense on tents and trailers.

Two bears investigate a culvert trap

Soft footfalls crunch on gravel. A black shape, darker than the forest shadows, stops at the edge of the campground, sniffing. Then it turns and steps soundlessly into a gap in the trees where a large culvert on wheels is parked behind a ribbon of yellow tape. The ripe, rich smell of dead beaver emanates from the dark interior.

The bear hoists himself into the culvert and grabs the bait at the far end. The door clangs shut, jarring the midnight stillness.

Another campground bear is going for a ride.

Park wardens and wildlife officers, who have to deal with the conflict that results when sloppy campers allow bears to develop a taste for human food, generally rely on culvert traps to catch the doomed creatures. More rarely, the officers use heavy-duty snares made of cable that catch bears by the feet, but, unlike ordinary snares, cause no injury. Snares work on animals too shy to enter a culvert trap or in too remote a location to place a culvert trap. Once officers snare a bear, they shoot it with a tranquillizer dart and then haul the unconscious animal away. Usually, if it's a black bear, they then kill it. In parks, however, and with most grizzlies, officers try to save the bear's life by releasing it somewhere far from where they caught it.

Too often, however, trapping and relocating bears doesn't work. Few places exist anymore where a bear that has learned to associate humans with food won't find more humans and get back into trouble.

Even if officers find a suitably remote area to drop a bear, they can't make it stay there. In 1995, in the Yukon's St. Elias Mountains, a hunter shot a grizzly bear released near Manning, Alberta. Bears have wandered more than a thousand miles from release sites, often returning home where they again get into trouble.

Bears often don't stay put because, in new terrain, they run into problems with already established local bears. If a new bear stays, it stands a good chance of getting killed. If it leaves, it also stands a good chance of getting killed. Moving a bear creates the illusion that you've solved a problem and saved a bear, but often the bear simply dies later.

surrounding landscape. Between 1950 and 1980 in Banff and Jasper national parks, wardens killed at least 523 black bears, and trapped and relocated another 547. The death toll in fact was higher because park authorities did not always keep records. Some harried wardens quietly dispatched and discarded spoiled bears.

The 1980s brought both new awareness and new technology to the mountain national parks of western Canada. Killing bears to solve garbage problems—never popular with park wardens—had become less acceptable to the public. In the early 1980s, park managers took several steps: they closed the Banff dump, enclosed Jasper's dump in a bear-proof electric fence and replaced traditional garbage cans with sophisticated new bear-proof dumpsters.

The Warden Who Cleaned Up Banff's Act

Eric Langshaw got the call at 2:00 a.m.: a grizzly was tearing at a back entrance of a large hotel near Lake Louise. Langshaw wanted to roll over and go back to sleep, but that wasn't an option. He was responsible for overall bear management in the Lake Louise district of Banff National Park and was the duty warden on call that night. He knew this bear well and he knew why it was being so aggressive.

"We'd had just one problem after another with the hotel and how they were handling their food scraps. We'd given them warnings, gone in and talked to them...I'd really tried hard to stop this but no matter what I tried, the issue would get as far as the hotel manager and nothing would happen."

Hotel staff, cleaning up between banquets, stored trays of food scraps outdoors for convenience. A large male grizzly bear picked up the scent one night and came down to investigate. Soon he was visiting nightly to scavenge food scraps as delighted hotel guests jostled to take his picture. Several times, stressed beyond endurance, he had bluff-charged tourists. Langshaw knew that the bear was now hopelessly spoiled.

"When we got there, we discovered that one of the hotel security guards had actually been firing his little .38 Special revolver to try to scare this poor bear," he says. "The bear was really agitated and we ended up having to shoot him on the spot.

"He just stood there and looked at us as we pumped one slug after another into him. It took five shots to put him down. He was just a beautiful old bear, the biggest I'd ever seen, and we had to kill him. Once it was done, everyone started heaping abuse on us, saying that all park wardens wanted to do was to kill bears and if we'd been doing our job it wouldn't have happened..."

Langshaw couldn't get to sleep that night. "I was thinking, 'how can we stop this from happening again?' It really bothered me that the park wardens got the blame for a problem the hotel management wouldn't solve."

The next day Langshaw assembled a file containing the management history of the bear, the warnings previously issued to the hotel and various other bits of information assembled over the

More recently, most parks have joined forces with neighbouring communities to build regional landfills that exclude bears completely.

Since the national parks converted their garbage management systems in the early 1980s, far fewer bears die because of garbage. Outside of parks, however, the garbage in some towns and settlements continues to tempt bears to death. A municipal landfill near Sparwood, B.C., for example, resulted in the loss of 13 grizzly bears in 1993. Two years later, conservation officers killed 60 bears in the same area, of which a third were grizzlies. The story at Revelstoke is even worse. From 1986 to 1995, biologist Wayne McCrory counted 106 grizzlies killed, or trapped and relocated, from the vicinity of Revelstoke's dump. "Many

The Warden Who Cleaned Up Banff's Act

eighteen months that the garbage problem had come to light at the hotel. But when he took it to his superiors, they told him that under no circumstances would they support him if he laid charges against such a powerful business interest.

"I showed the file to a friend in the RCMP," he says, "and he said I had a solid case that we could win. So I thought about it a bit more, and finally I took the file into Banff and got the justice of the peace there to sign the charges. Then I went back to the hotel and served the charges on the manager. He actually laughed, tore them up and threw them back at me."

Langshaw then left for a four-day vacation. When he came back, all hell had broken loose.

"I was put on suspension for insubordination," he recalls. "The Park superintendent and the Chief Warden called me in and handed me papers to sign withdrawing the charges. I refused to sign but I needed a reason, so I pointed out that the papers weren't in both of Canada's official languages!"

Shortly after, the case went to trial. The court found the hotel management guilty on all charges, imposed a fine and ordered the hotel to build a bear-proof garbage-storage facility. That legal decision made it clear that liability for any bear incidents would reside with whoever allowed bears to get at poorly stored garbage. It was a sobering message to Parks Canada management who at that time—the early 1980s—had not yet chosen a garbage management system to replace the old "bear-feeder" garbage cans still in use in most areas of the park.

"The very next morning I got a call informing me that I was going to be fired for insubordination," says Langshaw, who still shakes his head over the reluctance park managers displayed about enforcing Parks Canada policy and regulations. The warden got to keep his job, however, when the national media publicized his situation. Public pressure finally got Langshaw back pay to cover his suspension and cleared a reprimand from his employment record.

Parks Canada began installing bear-proof garbage containers throughout the park shortly after.

Bear Myths

1. When a bear stands on its hind legs, it's about to charge.
When a bear stands on its hind legs, it's simply trying to see or smell something it is unsure about. A bear about to charge lays its ears back and lowers its body closer to the ground, fixing its eyes on the object of its aggression.

2. You should be okay if you don't get between a mother and her cubs.
It's dangerous to get between a mother bear and her cubs. But in the case of grizzlies, in particular, you're risking your life to be anywhere near the cubs at all. It isn't your position relative to mother and cubs that makes a situation dangerous—it's whether the mother perceives a threat to her young.

3. Bears are dangerous predators.
If anything, bears treat humans as they do other bears. They rarely—extremely rarely—stalk people. They spend most of their time foraging for vegetables, insects and other food, not hunting live prey. By far the majority of encounters between humans and bears end peacefully. Like humans, bears prefer to avoid conflict. They can be dangerous, but that doesn't mean they usually choose to be dangerous.

4. Bears can't run downhill.

This myth probably comes from the way black bears look: lower at the front than at the back. It's dead-wrong. Andy Russell has measured between the tracks left by a grizzly racing down a steep mountain slope; some were five metres (17 feet) apart. Bears can run more than 50 kilometres an hour (30 miles per hour), and they can do it up, down or sideways. Humans can't even go half that speed.

5. Male bears will adopt orphaned cubs.

James Oliver Curwood's novel *Grizzly King* invented this idea, which the movie *The Bear* popularized. In the real world, biologists have observed adult male bears kill cubs when given the chance. Bear populations self-regulate in this and other ways, so that bear numbers don't exceed the available food supply. In food-rich areas such as the Khutzemateen estuary, however, Wayne McCrory has seen large adult bears co-existing peacefully with young bears.

A grizzly stands to gain a better view of its surroundings

6. If a bear charges at you, you should climb a tree.

Black bears climb trees frequently to escape danger, hunt insects or eat the buds and young leaves of poplar trees. The fact that you are up a tree won't stop a determined black bear. Grizzlies are physically capable of climbing and will do so if sufficiently aroused. They normally don't, however, so climbing a tree may be a good precaution for dealing with an upset grizzly.

7. Humans and bears can't coexist without conflict.

Charlie Russell describes three large brown bears that walked every day through a fishing village in Russia's Kamchatka Peninsula to hunt salmon below the villagers' fishing weir. Even the village dogs ignored the bears, although they barked aggressively at other bears. The bears, too, were discreet and respectful in their contact with humans. Many aboriginal tribes inhabiting Canada's west coast lived among bears all the time and developed a strong affinity for the animals. In western North America, most conflict between bears and humans results from poor waste management or ignorance of bear needs, not from any intrinsic problem with bears.

Black bear cubs at play

of those," he says, "were from the nearby national parks."

Reproduction

Bears are among the least productive large mammals to roam the wilds of Canada. Fortunately, other characteristics balance their low birth rate.

Bears live a long time—some more than 25 years in the wild—and have few enemies.

In theory, a male and female black bear born this year—if they bred as soon as they reached sexual maturity and as often as possible, and if their offspring did the same—

And Don't Come Back!

Relocating spoiled bears can work under some circumstances. Biologists in Glacier National Park monitored 22 relocated grizzly bears trapped and moved because of conflict with humans. They considered 16 of those relocations successful: the bears did not return or get into trouble again. All the bears they moved more than 120 kilometres (74 mi) from the point of capture remained out of trouble, while most of those moved shorter distances became repeat offenders. Females proved easier to relocate than males because they range much smaller areas.

Wayne McCrory feels that relocating bears would work better if wildlife agencies would subject bears to electric shocks, red pepper spray or other forms of negative conditioning to teach them to avoid humans. "It's mean," he acknowledges, "but it would save more bears' lives."

Most bear managers say that nothing works so well as simply protecting bears from the temptation of poorly managed garbage or livestock. Even so, conservation officers in B.C. spend up to fifteen per cent of their annual budget trapping and moving bears.

could in the space of 10 years have grown to a population of 15 bears, assuming none died. Grizzly bears are even less productive: in 10 years, a male and female born today could grow to a population of only eight.

By comparison, a pair of white-tailed deer born today could produce more than 1,400 descendants in 10 years!

Bears take several years to reach sexual maturity and then only breed at two- or three-year intervals. Where food is consistently abundant, bears mature earlier, produce larger litters and more of their cubs survive.

In Western Canada, black and grizzly bears both mate in May or June. As females become receptive to breeding, males pick up their scent and quickly home in on them. Males have a lot of work cut out for them, since females typically try to escape their attentions right to the hour when they are finally ready to mate. Other males, too, may try to cut in, leading to ferocious threat displays between the competitors and, occasionally, battles.

Once a female is ready, she may accept one to several males over the following week or so, and then the bears separate to pursue the equally important business of gaining weight for the winter.

The fertilized eggs do not implant on the wall of the female's uterus until she goes into her winter den late in the fall. Even then, if she is in poor condition because of illness, lack of food or injury, her body may just absorb the embryos. Delayed implantation acts as a sort of insurance policy for both female and cubs, allowing her to put all her energy into fattening up through the summer and fall.

The tiny cubs—small enough to fit into one hand—are born in the den late in January or early in February as winter winds howl outside. Black bears are born naked, grizzlies with fur, but all bear cubs are blind at birth and remain that way for the first few weeks, during which time they grow rapidly.

Endangered Bears

Animals become extinct naturally, but in the past century extinction rates worldwide have skyrocketed.

Bears Breed Slowly

	Age at sexual maturity Females	Age at sexual maturity Males	Number Of young/ litter	Years between litters	* Maximum theoretical increase from 2 in 10 yrs
Polar bear	5-7	5-7	1-3	2	11
Grizzly	5-7	5-7	1-3	3	8
Black bear	4-5	5-6	1-4	2	15
White-tailed deer	2	2	1-3	1	1,424

* assuming that the 2 were born in first year, and all litters had equal numbers of males and females that bred at earliest possible maturity, had largest normal litter each time, and there were no deaths.

The United States Endangered Species Act (ESA) became law in 1973. It had become obvious that without legal protection many plants and animals in the U.S. would slide into extinction. The ESA defines an endangered species as "any species which is in danger of extinction throughout all or a significant portion of its range." It defines a threatened species as one likely to become endangered.

South of the 49th parallel, fewer than one thousand grizzly bears survive in the fragmented wildlands of Montana, Idaho, Washington and Wyoming. Many of those bears live in isolated, islandlike pockets of habitat surrounded by human development—what bear ecologist Wayne McCrory calls "islands of extinction." Because of the small number of bears and the fragmentation of their habitat, the U.S. government has declared grizzlies an endangered species.

The ESA requires the U.S. Fish and Wildlife Service to come up with recovery plans for species formally listed as endangered and it prohibits

How Bears Die

When researchers killed most of the adult males in a study area near Cold Lake, Alberta, the bear population doubled, apparently because more cubs and yearlings survived to adulthood.

Male bears sometimes kill cubs and young bears—a factor that keeps bear numbers relatively low and that accounts for the aggression of female bears defending their young. Bear cubs are highly vulnerable, especially during the first weeks after they leave their mothers when they are alone, naive and often wander unfamiliar terrain.

Biologists don't know why adult males show aggression toward cubs. Some believe that by killing other males, the dominant male reduces the competition for females and increases the odds of passing on his own genes. A female who has lost her cubs soon goes into heat, increasing the odds that the male who killed them will get to breed her. Aggressive behaviour toward other bears also helps to keep population densities fairly low and bears well-spaced around the landscape, which reduces pressure on food supplies.

Under natural conditions, bear populations survive because a low death rate balances their low reproductive rate. It doesn't take a big increase in the death rate to change this balance and send a bear population into decline.

Food supplies vary from year to year depending on the weather and other factors. If the berry crop fails or something cuts off an important food supply, weaker bears may die of starvation. Others may wander far afield in search of food. Wandering bears may end up in farm country, near towns or along roads where people often kill them.

Where food supplies are particularly abundant—for example at a garbage dump, along a salmon spawning

federal agencies from taking actions that put those species at further risk. Most of the Western U.S. is public land and falls under the control of federal agencies such as the U.S. Forest Service, the Bureau of Land Management and the National Parks Service. This means that protection under the ESA can lead to restrictions on how westerners cut trees, graze cattle or recreate.

As a result, right-wing politicians and states-rights advocates have attacked the ESA. They resent the influence of federal agencies and eastern voters on rural westerners whose livelihoods depend on exploitation of public lands. They see the ESA as a symbol of uncaring outsiders who "put animals before people." A grizzly might reply that the charge lacks evidence: the continental U.S. has close to thirty million humans and fewer than one thousand grizzlies.

Horror stories about the ESA's impact on the economic needs of ordinary Americans rarely stand up to scrutiny. In the Pacific Northwest, for example, the northern spotted

How Bears Die

stream or in an area with many winter-killed animals—the antipathy of bears for one another breaks down and several may feed together, almost shoulder-to-shoulder. Normally, however, bears avoid each other because of the danger of an encounter turning ugly.

John and Frank Craighead studied grizzlies for almost two decades in Yellowstone National Park. They calculated that about ten per cent of the local bear population died each year because park rangers killed garbage-spoiled bears or hunters shot bears near the park boundaries. The grizzly population managed to hold its own until officials abruptly closed the park's garbage dumps in the late 1960s. Bears that had become dependent on the dumps wandered into campgrounds and towns in a desperate search for replacement food. They became problems and were killed in unprecedented numbers. As the death rate climbed above 20 per cent, the population began to drop alarmingly. Since the late 1980s, it has begun a gradual recovery due to cooperative bear-management strategies between the park and its neighbours.

Black bears reproduce faster than grizzlies and require less living space, so they can sustain a somewhat higher death rate. Even so, if hunting removes more than 15 per cent of a black bear population each year, the number of bears begins to fall.

Wildlife agencies regulate hunting, where they allow it at all. But they can't control poaching so easily, especially where backcountry roads and trails open up wilderness to motorized vehicles. Camps, dumps or permanent homes in bear country can also lead to high death rates in bear populations. Humans almost certainly mean garbage, barbecues, livestock or other tempting sources of easy food. Easy food, once a bear becomes addicted, is a one-way ticket to an early death.

owl—threatened with extinction by over-cutting of ancient rain forests—was listed under the ESA. It immediately became a symbol of all that was wrong with the act—animals before people, owls before forestry jobs. Analysis shows, however, that most job losses in the forest industry come from forest companies replacing people with machines and cutting forests faster than they can grow back. Many conservationists point to the spotted owl—and the beleaguered grizzlies of the Northwest—as reasons for the U.S. to retain and strengthen its Endangered Species Act.

Bringing the Grizzly Home Again

U.S. federal and state government agencies may transplant grizzly bears into areas where suitable habitat survives. In 1995, they successfully reintroduced wolves to Yellowstone National Park and wilderness areas in northern Idaho. The Grizzly Bear Recovery Plan proposes to restore grizzlies to Washington's North Cascade Mountains, Idaho's Bitterroot Mountains and Colorado's San Juan Mountains.

Idaho will likely be first. A state-sponsored committee of industrial, recreational and agricultural representatives proposes to establish an "experimental, nonessential" population similar to Yellowstone's wolf population. Critics, such as the Great Bear Foundation, say the plan won't work. They argue that the proposed recovery area is too small and that the extreme vulnerability of introduced bears requires nothing less than the full protection of the Endangered Species Act—something a "nonessential" population wouldn't get. Worse, they argue, the industry-supported plan will not protect habitat from clearcutting, road-building and other activities that harm grizzlies.

Jim Peek, who represents Idaho's Department of Fish and Wildlife Resources on the committee, points out that a comprehensive study identified large tracts of high quality grizzly habitat in north-central Idaho. Grizzlies once thrived in the area, but early settlers easily eradicated them—they shot bears that gathered to feed on spawning salmon. Peek believes the Selway-Bitterroot wilderness in particular has plenty of room for restoration of the great bears.

Peek, however, is one of the few unabashedly pro-grizzly voices on the committee. He says grizzlies don't have a lot of friends in official circles in Idaho. "The Governor's opposed, the legislature's opposed, the game commission is now opposed, and we don't know where the bears are going to come from." Even those in favour of reintroducing grizzlies to Idaho—local forest companies, unions and other interest groups—want residents to be free to kill grizzlies that cause problems. They also oppose special measures to protect grizzly habitat. As a result, national conservation groups such as the Sierra Club oppose the plan. The Great Bear Foundation and other conservation groups have proposed a

Bear Country— The Big Picture

Late March, and storm wrack is piled high on Long Beach, south of Tofino. The sky is gray, the air full of the smell of seaweed and salt. Waves sweep endlessly inland from the Pacific Ocean to break and race across the sands. Sand dollars and broken clam shells, kelp stringers and sodden bits of driftwood wash landward across the beach, then back toward the sea. They lodge in new-washed sand, breaking the ripples of retreating waves into vermiculated patterns that vanish as the next wave hisses in.

A squabble of gulls huddles around the rotting carcass of a sea

Bringing the Grizzly Home Again

different recovery plan for Idaho grizzlies. Their plan calls for a recovery zone more than twice as large as the industry-supported one and would include all the high-quality grizzly habitat that survives in northern Idaho's wilderness areas and public lands. The plan would also provide full legal protection to the bears and require rigorous protection for critical habitats.

A scientific committee that advises the B.C. government on grizzly conservation has asked to review any reintroduction program before the province agrees to cooperate in the transfer of B.C. bears to Idaho. The Canadians want to ensure that enough habitat is available and that any relocated B.C. bears won't end up shot and killed.

Bringing back the endangered grizzly will require biologists to release at least three females and a male every year for five years, but possible source

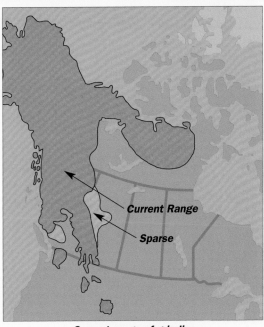

Current Range
Sparse

Current range of grizzlies in North America

areas—such as British Columbia, northern Montana and Alberta—all share the same problem: no surplus grizzlies. Peek remains convinced that a solution exists.

"If we can't have bears in this chunk of ground," he argues, "then we can't have bears anywhere in this country."

overleaf: Grizzlies must cover a lot of ground to find food

lion washed in by last night's high tide. Their keening calls echo down the empty sands, then erupt into a chorus of protests as they lift into the offshore wind, wheel in a tangled circle and land on the sand a few yards away.

The black bear that startled the gulls with his sudden appearance from the salal tangles at the edge of the beach ignores their bitter commentary as he follows his nose toward the stinking remains. He is three years old this spring and weighs 20 kilograms less than he did late in December when he excavated his winter den beneath an uprooted Sitka spruce. The moldering, fat-rich carcass will give him a big start on the task of rebuilding his weight.

As the bear begins to tear at the sea lion's swollen paunch, releasing a sudden stench of methane and rot, a wall of gray sweeps in across the breakers and up the beach. Icy rain pelts the impatient gulls and rattles the salal. Treetops vanish.

Thousands of kilometres of Pacific Ocean stretch to the west, a vast expanse of water spread beneath the sky. It brings the rain that drips from the feeding black bear's fur.

On the west slope of Vancouver Island more than a metre and a half of rain falls each year, mostly during winter. The towering rain forests of Pacific Rim National Park and the coastal watersheds of B.C. are products of abundant rainfall—those cathedral-like forests and the black

How Big Is a Bear's Home?

Bears don't have exclusive territories that they defend from other bears. A bear may occupy a home range that overlaps the territories of other bears and simply choose to avoid the other bears most of the time. A bear's home range can change in size from one year to the next, or from one area to another, depending on the distribution of food and other resources across the landscape. A human version of a bear's home range would describe an area covering our home, where we work, the stores we shop and our favourite recreation spots. Like bears, we tolerate the presence of other humans within our home range as long as they don't invade our personal spaces, compete with us too directly for things we want, threaten our off-

spring or belongings, or come into our homes without an invitation.

A male grizzly's home range covers an area as big as the greater Vancouver metropolitan area. A female black bear can use a home range half the size of Waterton Lakes National Park. Bears have to cover a lot of ground to find the food they need from one season to the next. This makes bears less abundant than most other large animals, even under ideal circumstances.

Bears have smaller home ranges in areas such as the B.C. coast that are rich in bear foods such as salmon and berries. Those that live in less productive habitats—the high mountains or the far north—necessarily range over much larger areas.

bears that haunt them get first dibs on the moisture that billows inland from the Pacific each year.

As the storm moves east, a series of mountain ranges forces it to rise again and again: first the Coast Ranges, then the Selkirks and Purcells and, finally, the Rocky Mountains. Each range of mountains trends southeast to northwest, almost perpendicular to the line of movement followed by the weather systems surging in from the southwest.

As the black bear gulps down hunks of well-cured sea lion in the sullen drizzle, the storm sheds snow on the high Coast Range north of Vancouver. Other black bears still doze there, beneath a metre or more of snow. They will not venture out of their dens for another month or so.

Further east, the storm has not yet arrived in the Selkirk, Purcell and Rocky mountains. It is late afternoon there, and bright spring sunshine slants down on the aging snowpack where it grips the steep lee slopes and leans out from the peaks in wind-sculpted cornices. As they have each late March and April for millennia, avalanches of sun-weakened snow thunder down gullies and lee slopes, following predictable paths between forested spurs. At the head of some avalanche paths, and in other high-elevation places where snow accumulates, grizzlies sleep, curled up, in snowbound dens. Near the base, beneath the hard accumulations of the snowslides, glacier lilies, spring beauty and other plants quicken, life stirring in bulbs and buds and roots. They will begin to sprout as the snowbanks melt in another month or two, just in time to feed awakening bears.

When the great weather systems of the Pacific break at length against the Rocky Mountains, the widest and highest mountain range of all, they have lost most of their moisture—and yet they retain enough to shed copious snow and rain on the high country of Yoho and Kootenay national parks and up to ten metres of snow each year on the Waputik, Wapta, Columbia, Brazeau and other icefields and glaciers of the Canadian Rockies.

Late March is still winter throughout most of B.C. and

A Bear's Home Is Big

Calgary:	1,200 km2 (460 mi^2)
Banff National Park:	6,640 km2 (2,560 mi^2)
Greater Vancouver:	2,800 km2 (1,000 mi^2)
Waterton Lakes National Park:	525 km2 (202 mi^2)
Home Range sizes:	
Grizzly bear (male)	1,000-2,500 km2 (385-965 mi^2)
Grizzly bear (female)	200-500 km2 (80-200 mi^2)
Black bear (male)	100-475 km2 (40-180 mi^2)
Black bear (female)	20-300 km2 (8-115 mi^2)

Alberta's high country. Beneath the blanketing snow, hundreds of black and grizzly bears lie asleep or stir sluggishly. Rabbit-sized bear cubs, born only a month or two earlier, nurse hungrily and fatten on milk twice as rich as human or cow milk.

East of Lake Louise, however, pigeon-toed tracks in the crusty late-winter snow of the lower Bow Valley plot the course of an old male grizzly bear who has wakened early. His worn teeth and an injured foreleg hindered his efforts to find food last fall and now he is sick and weak. His inadequate winter fat supply has long gone. He works his way along the railway line, head low, eyes dim. He will die soon.

A few other bears have emerged along the eastern slopes of the Rockies, early risers looking for

Trading Grizzlies for Wolves?

Fewer than 35 grizzlies survive in the North Cascade Mountains that straddle the international boundary between Washington and B.C. This dangerously small population may go extinct, if not from habitat loss in the short term, then from inbreeding in the long term. Even so, in 1995, the U.S. Fish and Wildlife Service cancelled a program to capture grizzly bears from other areas and release them in the North Cascades to increase the genetic diversity of the population. Instead, they spent the money to move wolves into Wyoming and Idaho.

Mitch Friedman of the Washington-based Northwest Ecosystem Alliance wasn't impressed. "I think the U.S. Fish and Wildlife Service is totally violating the law and its obligation to...throw a life preserver to a drowning bear."

The Fish and Wildlife Service continues to move ahead with a plan to reintroduce grizzly bears to Idaho's Bitterroot Mountains, where they're believed to be extinct. Meanwhile, the isolated Cascades population continues its dangerous slide toward extinction. Critics of the decision to defer plans to move bears into the Cascades believe that the Fish and Wildlife Service has bowed to the fears of some local groups who don't want more bears in their backwoods.

Chris Servheen, however, describes the situation as a "Faustian choice." He says both the Bitterroots and the Cascades are important, but his agency could get money for only one. A coalition of loggers, conservationists and other local interests has agreed to support reintroduction of bears into the Selway-Bitterroot wilderness, while local interest groups in the North Cascades remain bitterly divided. Local attitudes strongly influence the return on investment of any endangered species recovery program.

Friedman and others say the U.S. Fish and Wildlife Service spent money on wolf recovery that it should have spent on the North Cascades grizzlies. Wolves had already started to colonize the U.S. Rockies on their own without any help from biologists. Friedman warns that "endangered species politics may doom an isolated, international grizzly bear population."

winter-killed elk and deer, but most bears on the chilly east side of the Continental Divide still sleep, waiting for the warmth and greenery of spring before they venture out again into western Canada's bear country.

The remains of the Pacific storms break like waves across the Continental Divide into Alberta and spill down the valleys of the Athabasca, Brazeau, North Saskatchewan, Bow and Oldman rivers. They lose elevation, gain warmth and become warm, dry chinook winds that sweep onto the western edge of the Great Plains. The thirsty chinook winds suck moisture from the grassland soils of the Alberta foothills and prairies.

East of the mountains the Pacific Ocean's influence is weak beyond this chinook belt. Great weather systems that slump down from the Arctic become more important here in winter, and warm humid systems sweep north from the Gulf of Mexico in summer. Icy temperatures and sparse, long-lasting snows rule winters across the prairies, aspen parkland and northern forests of Alberta, Saskatchewan and Manitoba. Bears that rise too early here find no easy meals, only snow and hunger.

The Great Bear Foundation

One of the world's leading bear conservation organizations is based in a small town just north of Yellowstone National Park.

The Great Bear Foundation (GBF) designs and supports leading-edge programs to promote bear conservation around the world. In 1994, the GBF sent a research crew to Russia to meet conservationists and investigate the slaughter of brown bears by wealthy trophy poachers and traffickers in bear parts. The international profile that it continues to bring to that issue may help save one of the most productive bear populations left in the world. Closer to home, the GBF has helped B.C.'s Valhallas Wilderness Society lobby for a sanctuary for the rare white bears of B.C.'s coastal watersheds. In Montana, it pays compensation to the ranchers when grizzlies kill their livestock—more than $60,000 since 1985.

Four times a year, the Great Bear Foundation publishes a 20-page newspaper covering bear conservation issues from around the world. *Bear News* has received wide recognition as one of the most comprehensive, accurate and up-to-date sources of bear information in the world.

Great Bear Foundation
Box 1289
Bozeman, Montana 59971-1289
Fax: 406-586-6103
Phone: 1 800-822-6525
E-mail: greatbears@aol.com

Bear Country

1. Temperate Rain Forest

Along the western rim of the continent, and extending up the valleys of the major rivers, a broad band of temperate rain forest remains green and largely snow-free throughout most of the winter. Steep streams and surging rivers pour out of the interior mountains through lush evergreen forests. Each year, great numbers of salmon school at the mouths of streams not blocked by dams or fouled by too much logging, then surge upstream to spawn in shallow headwaters. Winters are brief, the land is lush and the streams provide reliable seasonal supplies of high-

Abundant moisture; lush greenery

energy food. This is bear paradise. Here, some of Canada's largest black bears and—north of Vancouver Island—grizzly bears thrive. Some inland rain forests compare with coastal forests in their productivity.

2. Mountains and Plateaus

Inland, the mountains and plateaus of B.C.'s interior and the western edge of Alberta lie buried under deep snows for four to seven months each year. Salmon runs penetrate some of the interior, where no natural waterfalls or man-made dams block them. The runs attract seasonal concentrations of bears. For the most part, how-

Avalanche slopes offer rich summer greenery

ever, black and grizzly bears that dwell in the interior mountains and plateaus rely on vegetation, insects and the occasional large animal for food. They travel through the short summer from one seasonal food concentration to another. Much of the landscape makes poor-quality bear habitat— continuous coniferous forest, rock, ice, human settlements—but pockets of abundance occur along stream bottoms, in burned and logged areas, on avalanche slopes and in the bands of interior rain forest that lie along the rainy sides of major mountain ranges.

3. Prairie and Parkland

East of the Rockies, winter snows are relatively light and a chronic scarcity of moisture restricts forests to sheltered places such as north-facing slopes out of the sun, high hilltops where temperatures and evaporation remain lower, and well-watered stream bottoms. Here, in the prairie and parkland regions of North America's Great Plains, con-

Pockets of shrubbery at the edge of the prairies

centrations of grizzly bears once struck fearful respect into the hearts of first peoples and white explorers alike. The bear country of the Great Plains now has almost no bears at all. A few pockets of grizzly and black bears hang on along the western edges of the plains where ranching country and protected parks offer some kind of haven.

4. Northern Forest

North of the prairies, aspen parkland gives way to the boreal forests of northern Alberta, Saskatchewan and Manitoba. Snow blankets these northern forests throughout most of the winter. Black bears and—in the Swan Hills of Alberta—a dwindling number of grizzlies sleep the subarctic cold season away. The boreal forest grows pine, aspen and spruce in a recently glaciated, rolling landscape of bogs, wetlands and twisting streams. Summer is short, hot and lush. Fires sweep the landscape each year, creating a complex mosaic of open shrublands, young forests and old forests.

A northern river floodplain

Lots of black bears roam many parts of this northern mosaic—the diversity of vegetation and abundance of water provides a bear-food smorgasbord during the snow-free season.

Black Bears

Curiosity not only killed the cat, it has proved disastrous for many black bears. Intelligent, curious, perpetually hungry, black bears quickly learn to exploit human sloppiness in their endless quest for energy-rich food. Humans, however, rarely tolerate the bears or blame themselves.

Black bears once ranged throughout the forested parts of North America, including most of the eastern half of the continent. They avoided the open, tree-sparse landscapes of the Great Plains, the high mountains and the arctic tundra—black bears only feel comfortable where they can climb trees to escape attacks from other bears. And most of North America's open country used to have other bears: grizzly bears and polar bears, which aggressively hunted their smaller relatives.

When European settlers arrived on the continent, they cleared openings in the great eastern forests for farming and timber. The resulting patchwork of habitats made living easier for the North American black bear, which found rich new food sources in the settlers' crops, domestic livestock, chicken coops and beehives. It proved a double-edged sword, however: more ways to dine, more ways to die.

Settlers hunted bears for food, trapped and shot them to protect farms and crops, and killed them out of fear. As settlement intensified and spread west across the continent, black bears began to vanish from many parts of their former range.

Black bears today occupy barely half of their former North American range. They no longer inhabit Ohio, Kentucky, Illinois or Alabama where they were once abundant. They have declined considerably elsewhere in the Eastern U.S. In most of southern Ontario, Quebec and the Maritimes, black bears survive only on land that agriculture has not preempted. All across Canada, where forest land and farmland intermingle, black bears suffer high mortality. Immigration of

Imagined Man-eaters

On a stormy day in the middle of an unusually severe winter, a black bear, hungry, no doubt, and seeking something to eat, came strolling down through our neighbourhood from the northern pine woods. None had been seen here before, and it caused no little excitement and alarm, for the European settlers imagined that these poor, timid, bashful bears were as dangerous as man-eating lions and tigers, and that they would pursue any human being that came in their way. John Muir writing about Wisconsin in the 1850s (from *The Story of My Boyhood and Youth*).

left: Black bears thrive best in forests dense with greenery

young bears from more remote areas largely sustains their populations.

Nonetheless, the range of the black bear in western Canada has changed little since the flood of European settlement first swept west across the plains. Island populations of black bears still occupy the Riding Mountains in Manitoba and the Duck Mountains in Saskatchewan, and the bears remain widespread and locally common throughout the northern forests and the forested valleys of the western mountains. The black bear remains the best-known and most frequently seen of the three species of native North American bears.

Black Bear Habitat

Black bears are forest bears, but they prefer forests with holes in them. Dense forest with little shrubbery or other understory vegetation has little value to bears except for shelter.

Few plants, other than mosses and ferns, can grow in the shadowed depths of dense forest. The most valuable habitats have tree canopies

For their size, black bears are suprisingly agile

Black Bear Facts	
Size:	1.2-1.9 m (3.7-6.0 ft)
Weight:	90-250 kg (200-600 lbs)
Description:	Black, brown or cinnamon; sometimes—rarely—grayish-blue or ivory-white. Appears higher at the hind end than the front. Has large round ears and a long nose.
Reproduction:	First breeds at three to five years of age. Has from one to four cubs every two or more years
Life Span:	20 years in the wild; some individuals have lived more than 30 years.
Food:	Plants, insects, meat.
Distribution:	Forested parts of North America, but extirpated from parts of the central and eastern U.S.

sparse enough, or patchy enough, to let sunlight reach the forest floor. A dense mass of greenery generally results. Bears are vegetarians, for the most part, and these green openings are like salad bars for them. In old-growth forests, aging trees that topple over create green openings for

black bears, and the rotting trunks of the fallen giants eventually become rich sources of ants, termites and other insect life.

Forest openings happen on a grand scale when wildfire roars across the landscape. Fire leaves scattered patches of living trees and

continued on page 66

Black Bear Food

Paul Paquet studied black bears in Manitoba's Riding Mountain National Park during the late 1980s. He examined the contents of 212 bear scats and 24 stomachs—enough to discourage anyone from considering a career in wildlife biology.

Many of the Riding Mountain bears fed regularly at the park's garbage dump, but garbage showed up in only three per cent of the scats and stomachs he examined. Paquet rarely found the remains of mammals or birds, though he did identify elk-calf remains in three samples.

Food type	Percentage of samples
Vegetable matter	100
Invertebrates (ants, other insects, etc.)	52
Garbage and debris	3
Mammals and birds	3
Agricultural crops	5

Bears concentrated on different foods as the seasons changed:

Spring: grasses, legumes, other herbs
Summer: insects, berries, grasses
Fall: acorns, berries, agricultural crops such as oats

Further west, a food-habits study of black bears near Cold Lake, Alberta found a similar pattern of changing seasonal foods. In this northern forest, however, unlike in Riding Mountain, the bears ate a lot of blueberries instead of acorns, a function of what was available and good.

British Columbia black bears have similar seasonal foraging patterns except in coastal watersheds with salmon runs during late summer and fall. Like the larger grizzly, black bears congregate to hunt spawning salmon or scavenge on their remains.

In the Alberta Rockies, research also reveals that bears eat different things in different seasons, but again the diet differs because of different vegetation and habitats:

Early Spring	Late Spring	Summer	Late Summer	Fall
forbs	cow parsnip	ants	raspberry	bearberry
bearberry	forbs	buffaloberry	ants	bog cranberry
horsetail	ants	buffaloberry	wasps	
carrion	carrion	forbs		

overleaf: Black bear cubs tag along close behind their mother

When Is a Black Bear White?

Kermode bear: like a ghost of the coastal rainforest

Ghostlike, surreally beautiful and rare, the Kermode or spirit bear haunts the coastal rain forests near Terrace, on Princess Royal Island, and in a few other parts of British Columbia.

Biologists once considered the Kermode a unique species, but then decided it was a subspecies of the black bear. They now know the Kermode isn't even a subspecies— spirit bears can turn up anywhere black bears occur.

Genetic research has identified the ghost bear as a rare colour phase that results when two normal black bears, each with the same recessive gene, breed. Some black bear litters contain both black cubs and white cubs: only cubs that receive the gene from both parents develop white fur.

Biologist Charlie Russell, author of *Spirit Bear,* a fascinating book on the Kermodes of Princess Royal Island, has even seen a white-phase "Kermode" grizzly in Waterton Lakes National Park. Wayne McCrory points out that grizzlies in the West Kootenays of B.C. sometimes exhibit a rare, white colour phase. He says these bears have Siamese-cat-like faces, white bodies and black leggings.

Kermode bears occur regularly only in the few bear populations where many individuals carry the Kermode gene. More than 10 per cent of the black bears on Princess Royal Island, and nearby islands and mainland watersheds, carry the gene.

"I will perish of disappointment..."

Dr. William Hornaday, the ambitious director of the New York Zoological Society, really wanted a white bear for his zoo. A New York fur trader had told him in 1900 about the rare white bears and he set to work tracking them down. His investigations led him, at length, to a fur dealer in Port Essington, B.C. The dealer wrote Hornaday that he regularly received skins of ivory-coloured bears from First Nations hunters in "...the district south of the Skeena River, sometimes as far south as Rivers Inlet."

Hornaday solicited the help of the B.C. Provincial Museum to help him get hold of a live specimen. When, in 1904, the museum took delivery of two dead cubs, Hornaday promptly declared the discovery of a new species and arranged to have it named *Ursus kermodei* after the new curator of the museum, Francis Kermode. It appears Hornaday hoped that bestowing this honour on the 30-year-old Kermode would secure the young curator's cooperation. If so, Hornaday hoped in vain.

Kermode finally managed to obtain a live white bear in 1924 when the B.C. Game Conservation Board seized a cub from a smuggler who wanted to

The Kermode is a rare white variant of the black bear

sell it on the black market in the U.S. Hornaday wrote to Kermode, saying, "If we don't get that cub, I will perish of disappointment."

He didn't get it. Instead, the poor animal spent the next 22 years in a cramped pen in Victoria's Beacon Hill Park, dying of old age in 1948.

Hornaday's regret was short-lived, in any case. After a prominent taxonomist from the University of California determined, in 1928, that the Kermode bear was only a colour phase of the American black bear and not a new species, Hornaday lost interest in putting one on display in New York City.

65

large tracts of blackened snags. No longer obscured by tree foliage, the soil soon erupts with greenery. Over the next several years, ants and other insects invade the wood of the dead trees. All the elements that add up to happy bears come together. According to Dr. Stephen Herrero of the University of Calgary and many other bear experts, our twentieth-

Spirit Bear Sanctuary

Princess Royal, 120 kilometres (74 miles) southeast of Prince Rupert, B.C., is part of a complex of islands and mainland watersheds that have the highest concentration of Kermode bears anywhere in the world. According to Charlie Russell, as many as one out of every seven bears is white in some parts of Princess Royal, compared to only one in 50 in the better-known Terrace area. A consortium of German hunters who have nonresident hunting rights to part of Princess Royal Island voluntarily agreed in 1994 to stop hunting bears to protect the genetic pool that produces Kermodes.

If western Canada's leading bear biologists and wilderness advocates have their way, Princess Royal Island will soon become part of a 265,000-hectare (655,000-acre) wilderness sanctuary where Moksgm'ol, as the Tsimshian people have long called the rare Kermode, can continue to live untouched by twentieth-century industrial development. The proposed sanctuary would also include Swindle and Campania islands, and three large watersheds on the mainland that support both black and grizzly bears. Its large size would protect not just a viable bear population but also the ancestral homeland of the Kitasoo people, and more salmon than all the other parks and protected areas in B.C., taken together, protect now.

For wilderness guide Charlie Russell, protection can't come soon enough for the bears he has come to know as friends.

Russell is somewhat like a bear himself—a powerfully built, slow-speaking woodsman whose gentle manner exudes quiet intelligence. Russell has studied and lived with the bears of Princess Royal Island for several years, developing strong mutual bonds with several bears. He has documented his experiences among the white bears in his book, *Spirit Bear*.

"My hope for the spirit bear sanctuary," he says, "is that it could be set up as an example of how we could get along with bears. Because definitely there is a real innocence there, with bears that had never seen people before. There was a clean slate. What we found was that they were very gentle with people, and they learned to trust us very quickly. We tried to maintain that trust by not doing the usual things that seem to cause grief with bears, things like letting them into our food and being aggressive with them.

"I would love to see us try a totally different approach—that we don't go in and start drugging them and hauling them around and putting radio collars on them and all the disrespectful

century success at putting forest fires out has resulted in the gradual deterioration of bear habitat in many areas. National parks and other areas now face the need to restore fire to the landscape, either by letting natural fires burn or by setting deliberate, controlled fires.

River floodplains provide excellent black bear habitat. Spring floods

Spirit Bear Sanctuary

things we usually do. I would love to see it just be a place where we're going to keep our food away from them—we're probably not going to camp on the island because that's a situation where they can get into food—and we'll just go there to enjoy each other."

Charlie Russell

Bears congregate along more than 60 isolated salmon streams in the proposed spirit bear park each August and September. Russell says that one tour operator, Ocean Visions, books small parties to visit the bears in early September. The tours have a conservation focus, which has impressed Russell. They respect the wildness and innocence of the bears.

"They're handling it very beautifully in my estimation. They're not encouraging the bears in any way to beg off them by giving them handouts, which is the usual temptation. I don't know why we don't seem to be able to relate to bears, or any animals, without feeding them or petting them or spoiling them in some way."

One cloud hangs over the future of

the area's black bears—their home is slated for clearcut logging. Logging has already opened up almost a third of Princess Royal Island. If logging continues, it will create new access for hunters and will damage forest habitat and salmon spawning streams essential to the well-being of the bears.

Charlie Russell, who will never turn his back on the bears, is determined that won't happen. And, as a sign of hope, he points out that public concern over the need to protect the spirit bears "…has already generated more letters than any other environmental issue in the history of B.C."

Spirit Bear Online

You can get in-depth, up-to-date information on the campaign to save the ecosystem that produces B.C.'s spirit bears from the Valhallas Wilderness Society or on the World Wide Web at http:/alpinet.net/~williams/spirit home.html

knock over old trees and create new green openings. The same floods often spread silt into low places and leave them saturated well into the summer, creating ideal growing conditions for sedges, horsetails and other prime food plants. Bears also find bird nests, frogs, salamanders and fish on floodplains.

Another, more problematic form of forest opening results when humans clear off the trees for agriculture. Agricultural crops—particularly oats and other grains—make excellent bear food. In some areas, black bears cause extensive crop damage. Beekeepers in the Peace River region of Alberta and B.C. frequently complain of bears that break into their hives—bears can't resist the unequalled richness of a feast on honey and young bees. Bears also scavenge the carcasses of dead sheep and cows that careless ranchers leave out on the range, which gives the bears a taste for mutton and beef. Sheep and young cows have no brains when it comes to avoiding predators, so black bear predation on livestock can become a chronic problem if ranchers

Bears of Many Colours

A black bear can be blue, brown, blonde, white or black. It's confusing. Some biologists have suggested renaming the black bear the "American bear" or some other name that avoids any mention of colour at all.

The name, and the confusion, originated when European explorers first ventured inland from the Atlantic coast. The bears they encountered in the lush deciduous forests were black, the dominant colour phase in eastern North America. The name "black bear" was well-established by the time settlers, spreading west across the continent, began to run into brown variants of *Ursus americana*.

Montana bear biologist Charles Jonkel speculates that the prevalence of one colour or another in different parts of the black bear's range may relate to environmental variation. Brown-phase bears are quite common in the Rocky Mountains and the drier regions of western North America, where bears often feed on open, south-facing slopes early in the spring. Jonkel has observed that lighter-coloured bears seem to feed on these exposed habitats longer than black ones, perhaps because they don't heat up as rapidly in the intense spring sunshine. Over the course of many bear generations, perhaps brown bears, on average, do better than black ones in those environments.

Every year, many visitors to the western national parks mistake brown-phase black bears for grizzly bears. It doesn't help that many grizzlies are not grizzled and range in colour from blonde to almost black, although grizzlies show far less variability than black bears.

Blue (glacier) and white (Kermode) colour phases turn up in black bears that live in some parts of western B.C. and southwestern Alaska. Both of these colours occur when a recessive

fail to look for constructive solutions.

When agriculture, recreational cabins or second homes invade the forested habitat of black bears, the death rate of bears always increases. Roads built for logging, mining or other purposes have an impact too: they expose bears to more hunting and make more of them into roadkill.

Family Life

A newborn black bear is little larger than a hamster. Blind and naked at birth, young black bears spend their first three or four months of life curled up in a den with their hibernating mother.

Bear milk is considerably richer in fat than human milk, so the black bear cubs grow rapidly during their time in the den. By the time they follow their mother out into the sunshine in April, most cubs have grown to the size of house cats. Long-legged and awkward, bear cubs approach the adventure of life with boundless curiosity and playfulness. Most black bear families have only two cubs, but litters of three or four are not unusual.

Bears of Many Colours

Brown or cinnamon bears are common in the Rocky Mountains

gene from one parent combines with the same recessive gene from the other. The odds of this happening depend on how many bears in the population carry the recessive gene. Two normal-coloured parents, if they both have the gene, can produce white or blue offspring.

Blue-phase black bears—actually a pale slate colour—have become increasingly rare, possibly because of selective predation during the late 1800s and early 1900s by trophy hunters who liked the novelty of the rare "glacier" bears. By shooting blue bears, the hunters probably reduced the number of bears in the population that carried the unusual gene.

Unlike the larger grizzly, black bear cubs instinctively bolt for the nearest tree when threatened, climbing high into the branches while their mother takes a defensive position at the base. Female black bears do not generally defend their cubs as aggressively as grizzlies. Biologists speculate that the cubs' tree-climbing defence makes extreme aggression unnecessary. In any case, bears have little to gain and everything to lose from fighting wolves, humans or other bears. Given the choice, most bears will avoid the risk.

Nonetheless, female black bears will take that risk if surprised in open terrain that has no trees nearby, or if they find themselves separated from their cubs by another animal that they perceive to be a threat.

Black bear cubs remain with their mother for one to two years, learning how to seek out the foods that will sustain them through the seasons. Bears learn both from observation and experimentation. Mother black bears provide plenty of opportunity for observation. They supervise the cubs and discipline them when the cubs' experimentation puts them in danger.

Young black bears separate from their mothers during their second or third spring. Some, especially males, wander widely. Dispersing juveniles make up many of the bears that raid crops, wander into campgrounds and otherwise come into conflict with humans. They do this partly from inexperience and curiosity, but perhaps also to avoid older bears which frequently threaten or attack young bears. Young bears often end up using marginal habitat—such as human settlements and recreational areas—to reduce the chance of encountering mature bears.

Black Bear Society

If you go down to the woods today, don't expect to find a teddy bears'

Bears Like Honey

When Winnie-the-Pooh wanted honey, he only had to worry about getting the honey pot stuck on his head. For real-life black bears, a taste for honey can lead to the boneyard.

Bears and bee farmers have a long history of conflict in the Peace River region of Alberta and B.C., and in the fringe of agricultural land along the Rocky Mountain foothills and the northern part of the prairie provinces.

Wildlife regulations in the western provinces treat black bears as agricultural nuisances and allow farmers to kill them on sight. Farmers and beekeepers used to do this with such regularity that honey-farming became a perpetual drain on black bear populations in the 1970s. From the farmers' point of view, black bears were a perpetual and expensive drain on honey production.

Electric fences have solved the problem of bears and honey for most farmers—a solution that protects bees and bears equally. Inexpensive solar-powered electric fences became available in the 1980s. Few bears want to touch a wet nose to a hot wire more than once.

left: A black bear cub climbs a tree

Smokey the Bear

"Remember! Only you can prevent forest fires."

The bear with the ranger hat and shovel has sternly issued that warning to Americans for more than half a century. Trying to find someone who hasn't heard of Smokey the Bear is like trying to find someone who hasn't eaten oatmeal porridge. Generations of North American children have grown up with Smokey's propaganda echoing in their subconscious, imagining forest fires as environmental disasters rather than life-giving natural processes.

Smokey was born in 1944, part of a public relations campaign to encourage Americans to take better care of their fires. U.S. Forest Service officials, who wanted as many trees as possible to grow up to become two-by-fours, were convinced that human carelessness caused most forest fires.

In 1950, fire fighters in New Mexico's Lincoln National Forest found an abandoned bear cub. A photograph of the tiny bear licking the face of a little girl appeared in newspapers across the United States, and the cub was quickly christened Smokey, after "Smokey" Joe Martin, a legendary New York City fire chief.

Smokey, the real bear, grew old and died in a zoo in Washington, D.C.

He lies buried beneath a plaque in Capitan, New Mexico, one of the few black bears in history to receive a funeral of sorts. Thousands of people visit his grave each year.

Smokey the poster bear continues to live on, warning new generations of campers to keep forests safe from fire, if not from chainsaws. As a good public servant, Smokey no doubt keeps his personal opinion to himself.

Real black bears, after all, vastly prefer burned areas to mature forests or clearcuts.

picnic. Bears rarely spend much time in one another's company. Even so, a complex social system rules in black bear country. Unlike other animals that feed on vegetation, bears have relatively inefficient digestive systems. They leave large, smelly droppings at frequent intervals that advise other bears of their presence. Although black bears don't defend clearly defined territories, most live within a distinct home range. They steer clear of other black bears except when food is concentrated and abundant.

Bears very occasionally fight, sometimes to the death, to assert their dominance over one another. But they usually establish rank by threatening one another, displaying the size of their body or engaging in brief skirmishes. Frequently, a smaller bear will simply flee at the sight of a larger one.

Abundant food generally makes black bears more tolerant of one another. They gather in large numbers, for example, at salmon runs and garbage dumps. The bears still have a personal space that they defend, but the sheer abundance of food makes that space quite small. It's not quite a picnic, but it's a gathering of animals who know one another and know their own place in the social hierarchy.

Black Bears through the Seasons

A bear has detailed and specific knowledge of its home range. It can't afford to waste too much energy in its annual race to gain weight before hibernation. Black bears use a patchwork of habitats through the year, concentrating on different food sources as they come into season.

Black bears emerge from their dens as early as late February or March in low-elevation areas near the Pacific coast, to as late as mid-April in the Rocky Mountains and boreal forests. Early spring is a hungry time because little vegetation has sprouted. Bears usually continue to lose weight until well into June.

In early spring, black bears often forage on sunny, south-facing slopes where they find overwintered bearberries or scavenge for winter-killed deer and moose. The first green grasses and sedges often sprout right at the edges of streams or in open wetland meadows, so these areas also attract black bears early in spring.

In summer, black bears search for pockets of greenery in wet meadows along creeks and rivers, on avalanche slopes, in aspen forests and along marsh edges.

As summer progresses, they spend a significant amount of time grubbing ants and beetle larvae out of fallen logs. Late in July or early in August, with the first ripe blueberries, raspberries or other berries, black bears devote their attention to exploiting this high-energy food.

Fall is a critical time for black bears, the last leg of the race to store enough fat for winter. As the berry crop succumbs to the first heavy frost, food supplies begin to dwindle. Bears feed on spawning fish where these occur in reliable concentrations. Coastal black bears, in particular, hunt salmon during the annual spawning runs. Elsewhere, black bears turn again to greenery, which often persists near water, and they wander widely looking for gut piles and wounded animals left by hunters. Big game hunting in the fall probably gives modern black bears a reliable source of high-quality food in the last few weeks before they have to den up.

Black bears retire to their winter dens early in November when snow begins to accumulate or, in coastal areas, when winter rains begin in earnest.

Threats to Black Bears

Wildlife agencies have traditionally undervalued black bears. Until 1989, for example, B.C. allowed hunters to kill up to five black bears a year. In many parts of the west, the limit still allows two. Wildlife regulations let

Bruno Was Here

Bears mark or rub trees to leave a kind of calling card. They mark some trees next to heavily used bear trails again and again. Both black and grizzly bears exhibit the same behaviour, raking the tree with their claws or rubbing their backs on it. Bear trees seem to get a lot of use with the approach of the mating season. Dominant males may use them to warn off competitors and stimulate females to become receptive to breeding.

Black bears make another kind of bear tree. They grip the bark at the base of the tree and pull it back, peeling off a long, triangular strip. This behaviour has nothing to do with communicating with other bears. It's a way of feeding probably unique to black bears. Black bears eat the sap-engorged inner wood of trees in spring, often girdling several trees in one location. This sometimes kills trees which, as they decompose, become ant habitat and future meals for bears and other animals that feed on insects.

Bears can girdle many young trees each spring and it makes them unpopular with the forest industry, especially

A bear tree, peeled for the sapwood

in the Pacific Northwest. For many years, some forestry companies hired professional hunters to kill black bears. More recently, they have introduced artificial feeding programs to provide bears with a different food source during the short period each year when they forage on sapwood.

Photographers who approach or surround black bears risk being attacked unexpectedly

farmers and ranchers kill black bears on sight. When black bears start to forage on poorly stored garbage or poorly managed livestock, wildlife officers frequently don't even bother to relocate the bears. They kill them. For most of this century, Banff National Park, like most national parks, shot "problem bears" instead of properly managing its garbage and sloppy campers. That began to change in the 1980s when park officials invested in some basic bear-population research. They had never studied black bears before, despite managing them more intensively than any other animal in the western national parks!

The findings shocked park managers, who had always assumed they had, if anything, too many black bears. Fewer than 20 black bears remained in the Bow River valley. Problem-bear shootings and habitat loss from fire suppression and tourism development had begun to threaten the very existence of black bears in Canada's oldest national park.

Black bears can seem more common than they really are in places like the Rocky Mountain national parks, where campgrounds and resorts are scattered throughout the best bear habitat. Garbage and other wastes, unless vigilantly managed, continue to draw bears into developed areas well after their numbers have dropped perilously low. People who estimate bear populations from the number of bear problems or sightings in developed areas have little more than an index of human sloppiness.

Gallbladders, Claws and Crime

The Humane Society of Canada estimates that legal hunting accounts for less than half of human-caused

overleaf: Poachers may kill over 40,000 Canadian black bears per year

continued on page 81

Spare the Bear?

Keith Everts, a rancher near Beavermines, Alberta, relates the following story:

We lost two calves to a black bear the summer of 1995. We had moved our cows and calves a month earlier than usual to a quarter up on the ridge, because of all the wet and flooding that year. It seemed like the cattle, the wildlife and everything were acting weird because of the flooding, and I didn't get a chance to check that quarter out in advance like I normally would do.

Bev and I went up to the dugout a few days later to check the cows and we saw on the ground this little calf and his guts were out. I'd never seen anything like this before—the last time a bear killed a calf all I found was the ear tag.

I didn't have a rifle with me, so I drug him off into the bush and said we'd have to come back after we'd got the cows and shoot the little guy, because he was still alive but way too badly tore up to be sewed back up. When I came back later he'd died, so instead of dragging off the carcass I left it there so we'd see if it was a predator. Because since I manage those cows, I have to know what's going on.

I came back the next morning and found no sign of a predator. The carcass was still there. I went on up the ridge by a big fir tree and went around the corner…and there's another dead calf. This one had his hide peeled back just like a banana. And I look and there's the bear scat and tracks.

Keith Everts

I called Fish and Wildlife and got the local officer. He called in their bear specialist guy—I called him Rambo. When they arrived, we went to the other side of the ridge and right away Rambo gets out and he's got his rifle ready—he's on a hunt, eh? We got ready to head up, and he says, "No, no, everybody stay behind me, nobody should be going in there that doesn't have to if there's a bear." And I'm saying, "I've already been all the way up—hey, I'll show you the tracks."

When we get there, we look at the hide and then he finds the tracks and says it was a black bear. I show him the other one too. Once they'd skinned it, I could see the claw marks where the bear had swatted it.

They explained to me that once a bear's eaten calves, he'd probably keep eating them and they'd have to trap him. They wanted to put the trap on the top of the ridge. We had to get

A Rancher's Dilemma

Bears rarely bother cattle pastured in bear country

permission from my neighbour. I took the one officer, but not Rambo, and my neighbour said okay.

So they set the trap and the officer called me that night and he said, "Geez I forgot to ask you—when we kill the bear can we just leave it there?"

I hadn't realized they were going to kill the bear. And now I'm feeling like an idiot because I didn't want this bear to get killed. I thought we were just going to move it somewhere. But I'd made the complaint and now they had to follow it through. So I said, "If you shoot it, you definitely can't leave it there, and don't tell my neighbour you want to kill it," because I knew she wouldn't go for that.

So anyway, I told my family. And we ended up moving the cows. We made that decision.

They never got the bear. It was a sow with two cubs and she lived on our ridge all summer. She's probably the biggest sow I've ever seen.

We saw her several times, and we'd watch her. And yet, we have a lot of cows here too, and she never bothered them anymore. I think it was the flooding...and my management, because I'd moved in there earlier than normal.

And here, with Rambo and all, it was like everything was the bear's fault. I mean, sometimes you have to kill these bears, but I felt really bad because it wasn't all the bear's fault. It was nature, it was my management, and all these other factors. It's funny because when we moved the cows we only went over one quarter section, and that was all it took.

black bear mortality. Poachers— some of whom masquerade as legal hunters and bear outfitters—may kill more than forty thousand Canadian black bears every year for their gall- bladders, claws and other body parts, which they sell into a lucrative illegal market.

A Canadian Wildlife Federation report says: "The illegal traffic in wildlife has been likened to that in drugs, each being capable of yield- ing high profits. However, the small penalties typically meted out to peo- ple convicted of poaching and illegal animal trade make those activities much safer than drug dealing…"

Poaching poses the biggest sin- gle threat to black bears. The inter- national trade in bear gallbladders and other bear parts has made poaching a multimillion-dollar business in the past decade. As trade relations between Canada and the Far East continue to improve, more pipelines for the illicit move- ment of bear parts will open up.

Gallbladders sell in North America for as much as $20 a gram (more than $550 an ounce), making them worth more than many illegal drugs. In fact, gallbladders are drugs. They contain ursodeoxycholic acid, an ingredient in traditional Chinese medicines such as Fel Ursi. In the Asian marketplace, the processed products of a gallbladder may sell for as much as $50,000—almost twenty times the value of the equivalent weight of gold.

Keep Your Pants On!

Park Wardens expect to see a lot of unusual sights while on patrol, but Darro Stinson never expected to turn a corner on Jasper's Icefields Parkway and find two naked people huddled forlornly beside their locked car. The black bear studying them from the highway shoulder looked more curi- ous than hungry, but the couple obviously had more goose bumps from fear than from cold, despite the mountain climate.

Stinson made room for them in the front seat of his truck and offered his jacket to the young woman, who seemed a little upset with the whole situation.

Then he opened his notebook and took down the details with all the professional detachment he could muster.

It seems the young couple, over- come with the romantic ambiance of the Rockies, had decided to head into the woods to commune with nature. They became so engrossed that they forgot all about nature until a loud snort told the duo they were a trio.

They retreated hastily for the safety of their car, only to discover they had left the keys in a pair of pants aban- doned in the woods.

The bear, no doubt fascinated by the behaviour of these strange crea- tures, decided to stay and see what they would do next. Luckily—especially given the mosquitoes—a park warden was on duty that day.

The moral of this story: keep your pants on in bear country or keep the car keys in your hand.

left: Bears eat the sap-engorged inner wood of trees

Bear claws and feet end up as soup and ornaments supposed to enhance the power of those who use them.

The market in bear body parts has rapidly decimated bear populations in Asia and other parts of the world. It thrives in South Korea, Hong Kong (the main conduit for illegal gallbladders), Taiwan, Japan and China. In some parts of China, "bear farms" milk bears for gall—a lucrative and excruciatingly cruel process. Bear farmers hold the bears in tiny pens and insert steel tubes into their gallbladders. The bears survive this torment less than ten years, dying of infections and other causes at only a third the life span of wild bears.

"It's horrendous what the Chinese government is doing, what they're encouraging," says Charlie Russell. "They have ten thousand of these farmed bears and they want forty thousand. They encourage taking them out of the wild to stock the bear farms. The health of the animals is horrendous. It's just a sad scene."

Proponents of bear farming argue that one captive bear can produce enough gall in its lifetime to save 220 wild bears from poaching.

Internationally, illegal profits from bear poaching exceed $6 million a year according to the Humane Society. As recently as 1995, undercover investigations by Environment Canada, the RCMP and B.C.'s Ministry of Environment turned up 191 bear gallbladders and 84 bear paws in several Chinese businesses in Vancouver. Investigators know that, as in most organized crime, this barely scratches the surface.

Steve Peterson of the Alaska Department of Fish and Game says, however, that wildlife officers overstate the problem. "Some of those guys say the problem's so bad we're going to run out of bears in five years," he says. "That's just not true. If there were lots of bears being poached for their gallbladders, we'd be finding carcasses out in the woods with just their bellies ripped open, and we're not. Too many enforcement guys see a crook behind every bush."

In some accessible areas, however, people do find bears with their bellies ripped open. Poachers left a popular Riding Mountain National Park black bear in this condition at an isolated garbage dump. They

Prevention Is the Best Cure

Prevention is the best solution when it comes to staying alive in black bear country. Prevention simply means:

- Showing bears the respect they deserve—watching from a distance, moving slowly and leaving when the bear begins to change its behaviour because of human activity.

- Keeping all food, garbage or other items that might attract bears safely locked away, especially at night.
- Making sure your actions do not habituate bears to human foods or garbage. You can prevent attacks on other people and the unnecessary deaths of once-wild bears.

A black bear can run twice as fast as a human

had taken his gallbladder and paws, and left the rest of his carcass to rot.

The trade in bear parts continues to flourish for several reasons. The proliferation of logging and other roads gives poachers access to remote areas. The legalization of bear baiting in western provinces makes finding bears easier. Wildlife agencies have less money for undercover investigations.

In addition, several provinces and territories still allow the possession of gallbladders, which makes it difficult for wildlife investigators to prove charges of trafficking. "There is a flourishing underground trade in gallbladders," says B.C. bear ecologist Wayne McCrory. "It can't be controlled until the Northwest Territories stops allowing legal trade in bear body parts. Right now, trappers and outfitters in northeast B.C. just drive across the border and sell their gallbladders and other bear parts. Where trade is illegal, we need to see jail sentences and higher fines so people will start to take this seriously."

Monte Hummel and Sherry Pettigrew, authors of the World Wildlife Fund Canada book *Wild Hunters*, say that the illegal trade in bear body parts "...has already seriously endangered several Asian bear species, leading to concern about whether North American bears aren't far behind."

Charlie Russell agrees: "The gallbladder trade is the most serious threat to bears worldwide, and I don't know what we can do. Talking to the Chinese, it's not just a medicine. It's a status symbol. Emperors were the only ones who could afford this medicine but now there's a lot of people that can afford it in China, and they want it as a status symbol. It's like driving a Mercedes."

overleaf: When threatened, most black bears prefer to bluff than to fight

Black Bear Hunting

The World Wildlife Fund says hunting already threatens some local black bear populations, especially in areas where baiting is legal and backwoods roads remain open for public use. Biologist Wayne McCrory says that wildlife agencies regularly allow hunters to kill more bears than the safe maximum. He also believes that up to twenty-five per cent of the bears shot by hunters don't even turn up in kill statistics because they escape wounded and die later.

Hunting hasn't historically posed a threat to black bear populations. Some provincial game biologists, in fact, argue that hunting may even increase bear numbers under some circumstances.

Hunters kill more males than females: males wander more widely, have larger home ranges and make the largest trophies. Mature male black bears don't tolerate other bears, so game biologists believe that moderate hunting can increase the number of young bears that survive to maturity. A study near Cold Lake, Alberta supports this: researchers killed dominant male bears and found that the area's bear population had doubled by the end of the study.

Some wildlife managers believe that hunting black bears on a regular basis keeps bears from becoming aggressive and makes them more inclined to avoid human settlements. No scientific evidence supports this theory, however.

Hunting can kill too many bears if

What's Legal?

Province or State	Hunting of Black bears	Baiting of Black bears	Hunting with hounds	Possession of Gallbladders	Sale of Gallbladders
Manitoba	YES	YES	NO	NO	NO
Sask.	YES	YES	NO	YES	NO
Alberta	YES	YES	NO	YES	NO
B.C.	YES	NO	YES	NO	NO
NWT	YES	YES	NO	YES	YES
Yukon	YES	YES	NO	YES	NO
Alaska	YES	YES	YES	YES	NO
Oregon	YES	NO	NO	YES	NO
Washington	YES	NO	NO	YES	NO
Idaho	YES	YES	YES	YES	YES
Montana	YES	NO	NO	YES	NO

Poaching Prospectus

Estimated illegal kill of bears in North America each year	100,000
Cash price for an illegal gallbladder in Canada	$125-$225
Cash price for an illegal gallbladder in Asia	$1,250-$2,250
Value of a gallbladder's products in the Asian marketplace	$50,000
Number of bowls of soup made from one bear paw	6
Price for a bowl of bear-paw soup	$250

left: Because they wander more widely than females, male black bears are more often killed by hunters

hunters have unfair advantages. Roads, for example, make hunting too easy.

Tim Thier studied black bears southeast of Cranbrook, B.C. in the Yaak River watershed. Hunters killed 10 of his 22 radio-collared bears within a single year. Logging roads criss-crossed his study area—they gave hunters great access and made it hard for black bears to stay out of sight for long.

Closing unnecessary roads so that hunters have to walk may do more to protect bear populations than restrictive hunting regulations.

Unfortunately, most government wildlife agencies have no say about road closures—the final decisions rest with forestry companies, oil and gas companies, and politicians who get lobbied hard by four-wheel-drive manufacturers and dirt-bike enthusiasts.

Wildlife managers try to mitigate the impact of roads on populations of black bears susceptible to over-hunting by making hunting seasons shorter or limiting the number of hunters. But this does nothing about the more serious problem of poaching. Experts estimate that poachers kill two bears for every one shot legally by a hunter. Open roads act like self-serve bear dispensers for criminals, especially now that government cutbacks have made wildlife officers scarce.

Staying Alive in Black Bear Country

Movies, books and news media often portray black bears as lovable clowns—roly-poly creatures with a hint of a smile lurking at the corners of their mouths. They look harmless as they graze on dandelions and clover along the edges of national

How Many Bears?

The black bear remains the only species of bear not officially considered threatened. The World Wildlife Fund estimates that half-a-million black bears inhabit North America, with maybe three hundred thousand of those in Canada. Hunters kill less than one per cent of that number each year.

But these numbers are meaningless, created to satisfy public demand for statistics. No wildlife agency in North America counts bears in a consistent and reliable way. Most of them either provide best-guess estimates or extrapolate population densities from local, short-term bear studies. Some biologists call this "mystery math."

Black bears sustain hunting losses and recover from bad years better than grizzlies or polar bears; they occur at higher densities and breed more productively. Nonetheless, the black bear faces an uncertain future. Monte Hummel and Sherry Pettigrew, in their book *Wild Hunters,* suggest that hunting pressure on black bears in Canada is approaching, if not already exceeding, the maximum safe level. In the last decade, many western jurisdictions have legalized the use of bait to hunt bears, which has increased the number of bears hunters kill.

Bears produce fewer offspring than almost any other mammal

park highways.

But every harmless-looking black bear can attack a human in a flash.

People take more chances around black bears than around their much-feared relative, the grizzly. As a result, black bears have killed four times as many people as grizzlies in B.C. and account for more than 80 per cent of all human injuries and property damage by bears in North America.

In most cases, bears treat humans as they treat other bears. If a bear or human invades the personal space of a black bear, it will respond with aggression.

Usually, the bear will stomp its front feet or turn sideways to make its body appear bigger. Most black bears prefer to bluff than to fight. In rare cases, a black bear may attack a human because it feels threatened—when, for example, someone cuts off its retreat or comes too close.

Even a bluff charge can prove dangerous, as one tourist discovered on Banff's Icefield Parkway. Trying to get a good photograph, the man moved too close to a black bear, which suddenly stopped foraging and bluff-charged him. He jumped back, and was struck and killed by a passing car.

National park visitors find roadside bears irresistible. As the size of the human crowd increases, the intelligence level decreases. People in a crowd do things they would never dream of doing alone, and bear jams often produce incredibly bizarre human behaviour—fathers holding their children close to wild bears for photographs, photogra-phers circling behind bears, people even holding out their hands to be sniffed, as if bears were pet dogs. Surprisingly few serious attacks occur at bear jams—black bears are remarkably tolerant of stupidity.

Very rarely, black bears do prey on humans. Small children, anglers who remain still for long periods and solitary hikers risk these rare attacks most. The best defence is to hike or camp in groups, and to supervise children closely.

Don't play dead for a predatory black bear—you're just saving the bear some work! Treat any bear that openly approaches, deliberately stalks or tries to circle behind you as a potentially dangerous animal. It is not protecting itself—it wants something.

Retreat inside a vehicle or build-

A Tricky Meal

Bear meat is fine-grained and rich. Some connoisseurs compare it to pork. And like pork, it frequently conceals a deadly parasite: a small worm that causes trichinosis in humans. Thorough cooking kills the trichinella worm, but it can survive if in meat served rare. Virtually every polar bear ever examined has carried the tiny parasite, and at least three out of every four grizzlies. Its abundance in black bears varies from one area to another. Otherwise healthy bears have little trouble coexisting with the parasite, but the same can't be said for humans who ingest it.

Black Bear Survival

Bear biologists agree these measures would help ensure a future for the black bear:
- Banning the use of bait in bear hunting.
- Making possession of gallbladders, bear paws or other body parts separated from a carcass illegal.
- Physically closing logging roads, mining-exploration roads and seismic cutlines, and prohibiting their use by off-road vehicles.
- Protecting prime bear habitats from human development.
- Closing or bear-proofing garbage dumps and reducing bear access to garbage, human food and domestic livestock.

ing. Yelling, holding up your arms or otherwise making yourself appear dangerous may outbluff the animal if you can't retreat. Distracting the bear with something edible may give you time to escape, but it will also reward the bear and probably make it even more aggressive next time.

If a bear you believe to be a black bear stalks you and attacks, your best response may be to fight back aggressively and loudly.

Pepper sprays can add to your defences, but you need to have them ready at hand. A can of pepper spray tucked away in a pack doesn't help in a sudden bear attack.

Bear Baiting

Hunters normally stalk bears they've spotted with binoculars. The hunters scan open slopes, tangles of berry bushes and other likely feeding spots or, less commonly, still-hunt slowly along game trails in good bear habitat. It isn't easy. Well over half go home empty-handed at season's end.

Over the past decade a new, more surefire technique—bear baiting—has gained acceptance in most of western Canada. It requires little skill but offers more certainty of killing a bear.

Commercial outfitters particularly like bear baiting: it lets them offer their clients guaranteed kills.

Baiting takes advantage of the inability of most bears to resist easy pickings. Hunters set out barrels of food in remote forested areas a week or two before the hunting season. By the time hunting season opens, most of the bears in the immediate vicinity are visiting the bait station.

Biologist Paul Paquet watched 16 different black bears visit one bait station near Riding Mountain National Park over the course of four hours.

Paquet found that nearly all the bears in the 2,970-square-kilometre (1,150-square-mile) park visit bait stations just outside the boundaries. He also noted that when female black bears investigate bait stations, they usually leave their cubs behind. Hunters aren't supposed to shoot mothers with cubs, but many don't know how mother bears behave at bait stations and kill them unintentionally.

Bear baiting seasons correspond with periods when black bears most urgently seek food: early spring and late fall.

Teddy Roosevelt, George Bird Grinnell and other American sportsmen aimed to elevate the standards of ethical hunting when they founded the Boone and Crockett Society in 1910. They believed in "fair chase." They thought hunters who practiced sportsmanlike restraint and woods skills made better hunters and better people.

Bear baiting, which involves no chase at all, strikes many hunters as unfair—the antithesis of what Roosevelt and others set out to achieve almost a century ago. It exploits black bears' inability to resist accessible, energy-rich food. To many, bear baiting doesn't even qualify as hunting.

Polar Bears

Polar bears grow bigger than any other bear in the world. Their elongated shape and small head give polar bears a distinctly different profile than other North American bear species. And polar bears, unlike blacks and grizzlies, are truly predatory—

meat makes up more than 90 per cent of their diet.

Polar bears hunt seals and other marine mammals on the pack ice all through the long arctic winter, heading inland to the arctic coast as summer approaches. They concentrate along the coast after the pack ice breaks up in June and July, then head back out to sea as the ice begins to form again late in the fall.

Pregnant females, however, remain inland, digging a den up to three metres (10 feet) deep in a convenient snowdrift. There, in a chamber that sits a bit higher than the entrance hole so that it will hold rising body heat, the mother gives birth to as many as three cubs sometime in December or January.

Polar bear milk is the richest milk of any of the bears, containing from 35 to 45 per cent fat. A regular diet of

seals probably has a lot to do with this, since marine mammals have heavy layers of insulating fat inside their hides. In any case, the cubs fatten, grow quickly and follow their mother out of the den in March.

Churchill, Manitoba—on the southeast shoreline of Hudson Bay—has one of the largest concentrations of polar bears in the world. An estimated 150 to 200 adult females den in the coastal watersheds between Churchill and old York Factory and along the south side of Hudson Bay west of James Bay.

Male polar bears, as with other bear species, kill bear cubs and smaller bears. Biologists speculate that this explains why pregnant females often migrate up to forty kilometres inland from the coast. By denning in marginal habitat, the

Polar Bear Facts (*Euarctos maritimis*)

Size:	1.5-3 m (6-11 ft)
Weight:	300-550 kg (660-1,200 lbs)
Description:	White, elongated body with a small head. Body is highest at the hind end.
Reproduction:	First breeds at four to seven years. Has one to three cubs every three or more years.
Life Span:	25-30 years
Food:	Meat
Distribution:	Arctic coast, Arctic and North Atlantic oceans, Hudson Bay.

left: Unlike grizzlies and black bears,
polar bears hunt throughout the winter

93

females avoid the big males that congregate on the best habitat closer to the coastline. Adult males can be up to four times larger than females.

Canada's polar bears form part of an interconnected population that extends all around the north-polar region of the planet. This circumpolar range means that Canadian polar bears are related to Russian and European polar bears.

Threats to Polar Bears

Egos

In the 1980s, people from many parts of the world became obsessed with adventure travel. The more extreme and demanding, the better. Several expeditions set out to reach the North Pole, or travel across the Arctic, or trace the routes of early explorers.

Polar bears are curious about people—they don't see many on the barren windswept expanses of the polar ice pack. Bjorge Ousland, writing about a Norwegian polar expedition in 1991, describes killing a curious polar bear that approached his camp. A few years later, another expedition killed four polar bears. As southerners continue to invade the Arctic, more bears will likely die.

Poison on the Wind

Scientists studying polar bears in the 1970s found high levels of PCBs, dioxin and other man-made chemicals in polar bear fat. It shocked them. We have since learned that global weather systems concentrate airborne pollution at high latitudes. There, plants and sea life take up the toxins and become food, in turn, for northern animals. Polar bears—the top predators in the Arctic—accumulate toxins that other animals have already accumulated. Toxins become concentrated in their tissues. Studies of other species show that the toxins found in polar bear fat cause cancer, other diseases and reduced fertility.

This problem will persist and grow worse as long as western society tolerates the release of synthetic chemicals into the environment.

Global Warming

Scientists no longer seriously debate the reality of global warming, only the nature of its consequences. Global warming comes primarily from too much carbon dioxide in the atmosphere, a by-product of fossil fuel combustion. The Arctic and Antarctic will feel the effects of global warming most according to every scientific model ever designed.

Global warming will reduce the extent of arctic pack ice and the length of time between freeze-up and break-up. This will reduce the time polar bears can spend hunting offshore. Global warming will doubtless bring other habitat alterations as permafrost melts and vegetation changes.

We don't have to pump so much carbon dioxide into the atmosphere. A carbon tax would create an economic incentive for industry and consumers to cut down on fossil fuels. Governments and industries with a vested interest in promoting the development and sale of energy resources have so far resisted any consideration of a carbon tax.

Is the Polar Bear A Grizzly?

Biologists, who normally consider two kinds of similar animals separate species if they can't reproduce with one another, face a strange dilemma in the case of the polar bear. Polar bears clearly differ from grizzlies—they look different, have different feeding habits and remain active all winter.

They also avoid grizzlies where the two species occupy the same territory. But polar bears and grizzlies cross-breed, although it rarely happens, and they even produce fertile offspring. That suggests we should class them as subspecies of a single, common species.

Wapusk

In April 1996, the federal government announced the creation of Canada's 37th national park: the 11,457-square-kilometre (4,424-square-mile) Wapusk National Park, among Canada's largest. It covers much of the Hudson Bay watershed between the Nelson and Churchill rivers. Wapusk is Cree for polar bear.

Conservation groups have praised the park for the important role it will play in protecting bears, caribou, historical remains, and breeding and migratory birds. First Nations and the governments of Churchill, Manitoba and Canada cooperated in planning the park.

Churchill: Polar Bear Capital of the World

Churchill, Manitoba—one of the most northerly sea ports in North America—sometimes seems to have as many polar bears as people.

Polar bears waiting for the pack ice to form frequently wander through town. When they find food or garbage, they can become aggressive. Some bears even prey on humans. Churchill has an innovative solution: it incarcerates these bears in pens in a large warehouse. When the sea ice freezes, it lets the bears go.

Once considered a nuisance, Churchill's seasonal gathering of polar bears has turned into a valuable tourism resource. Visitors fly into Churchill from all over the world to go bear-watching. They travel in

Churchill's fourteen or so licensed "tundra buggies"—large-wheeled school buses that bump easily, if uncomfortably, along unimproved trails across the subarctic tundra.

Churchill gets two- to three-hundred tourists every year and they pump millions of dollars into northern Manitoba's economy. Churchill is often used to illustrate the benefits of ecotourism. Some tundra-buggy operators, however, travel well off approved roads to get close to bears, harass bears to get better photos and allow their clients to feed bears.

Nonetheless, Churchill—once one of the world's "black holes" for polar bears—now has a huge economic stake in keeping them alive.

overleaf: The best habitat for polar bears is close to the arctic coastline

Grizzly Bears

T he dancing bears of medieval circuses, and the chained bears that fought and died to entertain English nobility, were the same species as North America's silvertip grizzlies and Kodiak bears. The grizzly belongs to the most widely distributed species of bear in the world—*Ursus arctos*, the brown bear. *Ursus arctos* ranges from the Pyrenees and Alps of Europe all across Asia, through parts of China and Japan, to Siberia, Alaska and down the western half of North America to Wyoming.

Some taxonomists argue that the Eurasian and North American populations are separate species, but most now agree that European brown bears and North American grizzly bears are both *Ursus arctos*.

Most North American grizzlies belong to the subspecies *Ursus arctos horribilis*, descended from brown bears that colonized this continent about fifteen thousand years ago across the Bering land bridge from Siberia. Two other subspecies—perhaps descended from brown bears that arrived in North America forty thousand years ago—live in Alaska. *U.a. gyas* occupies the coastal watersheds of mainland Alaska, and *U.a. middendorffi*—the famous Kodiak bear which can grow as large as 600 kilograms (1,400 pounds)—inhabits Kodiak, Afognak and Shuyak Islands.

The various subspecies of *Ursus arctos* once ranged even more widely than they do today. Brown bears lived in Ireland until about 750 A.D. and survived in Great Britain for another two or three centuries. They survived in the dark forests of Germany until the late 1700s and in the Swiss and French Alps until early in the twentieth century.

By that time, North American grizzly populations had started to shrink. By the beginning of the twentieth century, few plains grizzlies remained. They had once ranged down the river valleys of the Great Plains all the way east to what is now Western Ontario and south along the Mississippi Valley. California may at one time have had the highest concentration of grizzlies in North America, with an estimated population of ten thousand bears. The last survivors were finally killed in the early 1920s, leaving the Golden Bear State without any golden bears.

Grizzly Habitat

The grizzly is a creature of the whole landscape. He doesn't have just one habitat—he has many. Life-renewing natural processes such as fire, flood and avalanche often create the most productive and important parts of a grizzly's home range. A landscape where dams have tamed the rivers, or where wild fire no longer sweeps the land, does not look as much like home to a grizzly bear as a landscape

left: A grizzly guards its territory

where natural forces rule.

Along the west coast, grizzlies forage in old-growth temperate rain forest, with its many small clearings and lush understory. In the interior mountains and plateaus, they prefer burned forest, where berries grow in abundance, ants thrive in rotting logs and sweetvetch roots spread through the sun-warmed soil. They wander

The Plains Grizzly

David Thompson, the great mapmaker and explorer of the early nineteenth century, encountered grizzly bears from the time he reached the Saskatchewan River—well out on the prairies—and throughout his explorations of Western Canada.

Fifty years later, the Palliser expedition ran into grizzly bears along the lower Red Deer River and near present-day Medicine Hat, far east of where they occur today. John "Kootenai" Brown, an adventurer who later became the first park warden in Waterton Lakes National Park, wrote that when he first arrived in the region in 1865 "...there roamed all along the south branch of the Saskatchewan River hundreds of grizzly bear, small grizzlies, but grizzlies just the same."

The world of the plains grizzly was one of great abundance: millions of bison, countless elk and antelope, thickets of berry-producing shrubs, roots and lush vegetation along wild prairie rivers. The great bears probably spent most of their time in the cottonwood forests and shrubbery along rivers, streams and coulees, and in the shrubby draws and forests of the Cypress, Sweetgrass and Neutral hills. They ranged as far east as Manitoba—even into parts of Ontario—and south as far as western Oklahoma and Texas. In the eastern part of their range, grizzlies fed on oak mast, wild grapes and other seasonal foods not available in the west.

The original people of the Great Plains feared and respected the grizzly. Until traders arrived with metal arrowheads, and later with firearms, first peoples had no effective protection against the great bears.

The hunting methods of the Siksika, Piikanii, Kainai and other tribes put them in frequent danger from grizzly bears. These tribes relied heavily on the plains bison for food. They often chased bison in large numbers off cliffs, or into traps known as buffalo pounds, or into deep snowdrifts. There they slaughtered all they could and camped near the carcasses until they had finished stripping them of meat, hides and other products. Grizzlies, strongly attracted to carcasses, must have gravitated to the kill sites. Many early explorers' journals describe grizzlies scavenging on bison remains along prairie rivers.

First Nations people also relied heavily on saskatoons and other berries. This put the women who gathered them in potential conflict with grizzly bears, which relied on the same seasonal food source.

Artist Paul Kane, camped among the Cree near Fort Edmonton in 1845, wrote that: "There is no animal on the

along flood-scarred river flats, fishing for spawning salmon or trout in season, digging roots or grazing on succulent hairgrass. They venture up meltwater gullies eating horsetail foliage, then wander onto avalanche slopes where they find abundant green vegetation, berries and, in spring, sometimes an avalanche-killed elk or mountain goat.

The Plains Grizzly

whole continent that the Indians hold in so much dread as the grisly bear, and few will attack one of them alone, unless with a very fleet horse under him..."

The repeating rifle and strychnine, both of which arrived in Western Canada in the early 1870s, brought the reign of the great bear to a sudden end. One trading post near the Cypress Hills took in 750 "grizzle" hides in a single year. Commercial hunting had eradicated grizzlies from the plains by the late 1800s.

A few grizzlies still dwell in part of the plains grizzly's former range—in Montana's Pine Butte Nature Preserve and Blackfeet Indian Reservation, and along the eastern edge of the Waterton-Glacier International Peace Park. They live year-round in the river-bottom willow thickets, and intermingled bunchgrass prairie and aspen bluffs, that spill east from the Rocky Mountains.

From Mexico north, European settlement of the American West filled valleys with livestock, farms, towns and railroads. It fragmented grizzly habitat and pushed the bears into isolated, island like mountain ranges. There, hunters—white and native alike—killed them mercilessly for the fur trade. Ranchers invaded their habitat and killed them when the bears learned to hunt cattle and sheep. One by one, as these "island" populations dwindled below the point where they could recover, grizzly populations winked out.

Arizona's last grizzly was killed in 1935. The last known Mexico grizzly was shot in 1965, although a few optimistic biologists persist in the hope that a small population may survive in the Sierra Madre. A bow hunter killed Colorado's last grizzly in 1979, a quarter century after most experts thought the bear had been extirpated from that state. New Mexico, Utah, Nevada, Oregon—most western states have only the ghosts of grizzlies left.

Small islands of grizzlies hang on in the Greater Yellowstone ecosystem where Montana, Idaho and Wyoming abut one another, and in three other isolated mountain ranges in northern Montana. Biologists estimate that half of Canada's grizzlies survive in British Columbia. Even there, hydroelectric reservoirs, towns and agricultural development isolate many grizzly subpopulations that face a growing risk of dying out, one by one.

COSEWIC—the Committee on the Status of Endangered Wildlife in Canada—concluded in an exhaustive 1990 review of the grizzly bear's status that human activity threatens more than 60 per cent of grizzly habitat.

overleaf: Adult grizzlies are mainly solitary animals

Some human activities create habitats that resemble natural habitats.

Logging, for example, removes forest canopy just like fire. Logged areas—until replanted trees start to shade the soil—grow lots of huckleberries and other bear foods. Unlike fire, however, logging removes most of the tree trunks that would otherwise have fallen over and become ant habitat. It leaves few patches of standing trees to provide bears with shelter and safety. Worse, some forestry companies use herbicides to kill plants they feel compete with commercial tree species, even though bears depend on these plants.

Logging roads pose more problems. When the loggers go home, the roads remain open to hunters, berry pickers and mountain bikers. Studies have shown that when road densities exceed one kilometre for every square kilometre of landscape, as they do in many logged watersheds, grizzly deaths from legal and illegal killing rise. They also show that grizzly densities drop because the surviving bears avoid feeding near the roads.

Ski hills create another artificial habitat, one that resembles avalanche slopes. But ski hills rarely achieve their potential for grizzly bears. Most ski-hill operators encourage people to hike and bike the runs during summer, and many people don't know how to coexist with bears or don't want to.

Floods, fires, avalanches and low human use translate into high-quality grizzly habitat. Roads, garbage and high human use translate into poor grizzly habitat. For the most part, grizzlies continue to thrive only

Japan's Grizzlies

Four times as many *Ursus arctos* now live in the wild in Japan—on the island of Hokkaido—than survive in the continental U.S.A. The bears, native to that country, live in forested coastal areas and are frequently killed to protect farms or to supply the gallbladder trade.

Grizzly Facts *(Ursus arctos horribilis)*

Size:	1.8-2.5 m (5.5-7.5 ft)
Weight:	130-400 kg (280-900 lbs). Kodiaks grow larger.
Description:	Brown, ranging from almost blonde to almost black, often with a grizzled appearance on the back, shoulders and head. Pronounced hump at front shoulders, long claws on forefeet, and a dish-shaped face with small ears.
Reproduction:	First breeds at five to seven years and has one to three cubs every three or more years.
Life Span:	25 years
Food:	Plants, insects, meat.
Distribution:	Northern U.S. Rockies, extreme western Alberta, most of B.C., and Alaska east to Hudson Bay.

A grizzly mother suckling her cubs

in large parks and wilderness areas with few roads and little development. The United States Forest Service has recently begun to close and reclaim roads in some national forests, turning logged areas into useful habitat for grizzlies and other sensitive species.

Alberta and B.C. have, so far, failed to take these progressive steps. The Canadian approach more often consists of posting signs that prohibit travel on industrial roads, trusting poachers to obey!

Family Life

Female grizzlies are fiercely protective mothers. They need to be. Grizzly bears have the lowest reproductive rate of any North American mammal. A female grizzly will reach five or more years of age before breeding. Then, if all goes well, she will produce only two or three cubs every three years.

The tiny, blind cubs—about the size of a shoe—are born in midwinter while their mother hibernates. For the first few months, they live a confined and comfortable life of nursing, warmth and nurture inside their birth den. In April, they emerge, blinking, into their first high-country spring. They begin an intense education in the life skills that must serve them throughout their lives. They also begin the most dangerous part of their lives. Far more young grizzlies die than adults.

The cubs spend two or three years with their mother, denning with her each winter and following her around her home range. This extended childhood allows their mother to teach them about seasonal foods and to protect them until they have

grown to nearly adult size. Wolves and cougars prey on cubs, but the greatest danger they face may well be their father—male grizzlies sometimes harass or kill cubs and young bears. Female grizzlies with cubs often use higher elevations and more marginal habitat than males to reduce the risk of a confrontation.

Cubs play with one another and their mother a great deal during the first year, clearly demonstrating both affection and enjoyment. The bond between siblings may survive for years, well after they have separated to adopt the solitary life typical of adult grizzlies.

Social Life

Adult grizzlies don't appear to have much of a social life. The only time one grizzly spends much time in the company of another is during mating season and even that seems a reluctant affair, at least on the part of the female. I once watched a female with two yearlings spend most of a week clambering around in cliffs that would challenge a mountain goat, peering down into the timber where a large male lurked hopefully.

Males will travel great distances in late spring searching for breeding-age females. If they find a female with cubs, they may try to isolate her from her offspring—it's often during the mating season that females finally separate from their young.

Once a male finds a female in heat, he shadows her constantly. As she reaches the receptive stage of

Death Cry

A few days after our arrival, the death cry was given...The cry was from a young man who held his bow and arrows, and showed one of his thighs torn by a grizzled bear...which had killed two of his companions. The old man called for his powder horn and shot bag, and, seeing the priming of his gun in good order, he set off with the young man for the bear, which was at a short distance. They found him devouring one of the dead. The moment he saw them he sat up on his hind legs, showing them his teeth and long clawed paws. In this, his usual position to defend his prey, his head is a bad mark, but his breast offers a direct mark to the heart, through which the old man sent his ball and killed him.

The two young men who were destroyed by the bear had each two iron-shod arrows, and, the camp being near, they attacked him for his skin and claws, but unfortunately their arrows stuck in the bones of his ribs, and only irritated him...

The first poor fellow was still alive, and knew his parents, in whose arms he expired. The bear, for the mischief he had done, was condemned to be burnt to ashes. The claws of his forepaws, very sharp and long, the young man wanted for a collar but it was not granted; those that burned the bear watched until nothing but ashes remained.

David Thompson, 1787, near the present site of Calgary.

left: B.C. hunters kill between 200 and 400 grizzlies each year

her cycle, he herds her into some isolated area and holds her there until finally she is ready to mate. In the Rockies, male grizzlies sometimes corral females on mountain ridges.

Grizzlies mate repeatedly over a period of days before the two animals suddenly lose interest in each other. Another brief mating period may follow a few weeks later, but by the end of June the bears are on their own again.

Males wander much more widely than females, marking their home ranges with droppings, urine and marker trees. Observant hikers can find marker trees along several hiking trails in the Rocky Mountain national parks. The trees have tell-tale tufts of hair stuck in the bark, claw marks and smooth surfaces from repeated rubbing.

When bears meet, they quickly establish dominance by posturing, bluff charging or threatening one another. The underdog soon takes to his heels. If he doesn't, a fight may follow. The bears roar and grip one another, biting at each other's jaws and head until one surrenders or suffers mortal injuries.

Grizzlies don't tolerate one another well, probably because they have to compete for scarce and patchily distributed food. The landscape just can't hold a lot of grizzlies—one of the reasons they are relatively rare even at the best of times. Abundant food, however, makes grizzlies more willing to put up with close neighbours.

Along some coastal salmon streams, large numbers of grizzly bears sometimes share the rich harvest of spawning fish. At Alaska's McNeill River Falls, visitors can see as many as fifty grizzlies feeding together during the annual salmon run. Until Banff, Yellowstone and other national parks closed their garbage dumps in the early 1970s, similar congregations of grizzlies took advantage of these artificial windfalls.

But even when grizzlies congregate to share abundant food, they display an obvious social hierarchy: smaller or younger bears usually give way to the dominant bears and settle for the less desirable feeding stations.

Grizzly Bears through the Seasons

Early in April, grizzlies wake from their winter's sleep and venture out of their dens into the blinding glare of spring sunlight. Snow still blankets the high mountain slopes of Western Canada, but the sun's growing warmth has started to break up the snowpack. Avalanches thunder through the spring afternoons as the melting snow crashes down gullies into the valleys below.

The bears are hungry, but food is in short supply. Most trees and shrubs won't leaf for another month and only the grass at the lowest elevations has begun to green up.

In spring, grizzlies gravitate to sunny, south-facing slopes or the banks of low-elevation creeks and rivers. There, where the snow has melted away and revealed the matted brown of last year's grasses, their sensitive noses sniff out sweet-vetch roots, glacier lily bulbs and

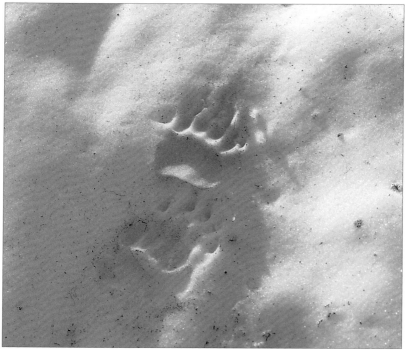

Grizzly tracks in the snow

other buried treasures. The bears' long claws efficiently uproot the starch-rich foods.

Coastal grizzlies find a milder reception, especially along low-elevation river valleys. They feed on the roots of skunk cabbage and sedges or, where they can find them, the well-cured carcasses of salmon that died the previous fall after spawning.

All the time, the grizzlies' noses test the mountain breeze for the promise of heartier fare. Late winter is a time of death for deer, elk, bighorn sheep and other animals. Some die in spring avalanches; others melt out of snowdrifts where the winter buried them. For a hungry grizzly, roots are fine but carrion is a jackpot.

The snowpack diminishes and the days lengthen. New greenery begins to sprout. The bears continue to dig roots and bulbs around the shrinking snowdrifts, but now they begin to add highly nutritious young grass, horsetails and other sprouting vegetation to their diet.

By late May, the bears have given up glacier lilies, sweetvetch and other roots and bulbs whose store of starch has gone into producing new stems, leaves and flowers. A lush variety of new greenery now surrounds the grizzlies. Life is one endless salad interrupted by the occasional duck nest or other unexpected side dish.

Threats to Grizzlies

Grizzly bears need space. But

overleaf: Young grizzlies leave their mothers after 2 or 3 years

The Cairn Pass Orphans

Park Warden Norm Woody spotted the female gemale grizzly too late as he rode into an open timberline meadow. She loped toward him, trailed by her three cubs. Woody thought she was just curious at first, but that changed when she got too close for a comfortable retreat and realized her cubs were at risk. She suddenly laid back her ears and broke into a full charge.

Woody's warning shots had no effect. At last, with the grizzly only a few metres away, the warden had to kill her in self-defence. Park wardens always find the death of a female grizzly hard to stomach. This death, in the summer of 1975, was particularly galling. Woody was part of a joint Parks Canada-Canadian Wildlife Service study intended to help grizzlies, not kill them.

Woody and his research colleagues faced a further dilemma: the dead mother had left behind three orphaned cubs barely six months old. Nobody had ever heard of grizzlies that small surviving in the wild.

After discussing all the options, the researchers decided to leave the cubs alone and hope for the best. They ended that field season with heavy hearts, worried that the incident may have brought death to four bears.

When the researchers returned to their study area the following May, however, they discovered all three cubs digging sweetvetch roots on a timberline knoll near Cairn Pass. The bears' small size showed they had endured a stressful first year of life, but at least they had survived. The bears

spent the whole summer in or near Cairn Pass, feeding mostly on sweetvetch roots, although on one occasion they stole a marmot from a coyote and spent almost an hour chasing and being chased by their victim. The cubs were inseparable and often hugged and played with one another.

In late August, one of the cubs disappeared, possibly killed by a large male grizzly known to sometimes travel through the area. The survivors appeared nervous and uneasy at first, but within a few days they had recovered their spirits and played and dug roots as if nothing had changed.

Next spring, the cubs were still alive, although noticeably smaller than other grizzlies their age. Tracks in the snow showed that they had spent the winter in the den where they had been born.

The cubs ultimately spent four years together before separating in 1979. By then, the researchers had gained valuable insights into the life of grizzly bear cubs and the impact on young cubs of losing their mother. The orphans remained attached to one another longer than usual. They were undersized, wary of humans, vulnerable to predators and reluctant to travel outside the limited area their mother had introduced them to. In late summer, they ate early seasonal foods such as sweetvetch roots and grass, although other bears in the area fed heavily on berries. Apparently their mother had shown them only these foods before she died.

A grizzly rests between meals

people—350 million of us on this continent—take up most of it.

Grizzly bears need more space than even the big western national parks and wilderness areas provide. Parks such as Banff offer less space than we like to think. More than 7,000 people live year-round in Banff National Park and another five million visit the park each year to use facilities, trails and resorts that take up space no longer available to the great bears.

The grizzly conservation problem has two dimensions: habitat loss and habitat effectiveness. Grizzlies lose habitat when humans take it for towns, mines or farms. Grizzlies lose effective use of their remaining habitat when human activity makes living there too dangerous or stressful.

Strategies to protect grizzly bear habitat won't work without parallel, but different, strategies to improve its effectiveness.

Habitat Loss

For the past two centuries, we have put the landscapes of western North America to work. Where the climate and soils would support crops, we have turned natural ecosystems into farmland. We have dedicated forests to wood production and grassland to beef production. We even expect the high mountains, where most large parks and wilderness areas exist, to contribute to the economy through the production of tourism revenue.

Even in parts of the landscape that seem wild, grizzlies can still run into ecological "black holes"—small areas devoted to human use where bears die because of conflicts with people. Alberta's Poll Haven Community Pasture, a tract of public land in southwestern Alberta, stands as a notorious example, along with regional garbage dumps not bear-proofed with electric fences or other means.

Grizzlies have always foraged at Poll Haven in early spring and late summer. According to biologist Brian Horesji, Poll Haven became a drain on the local grizzly population, which extends south into Montana and west into British Columbia, when the Alberta government decided to give cattle grazing precedence over other uses. Legal and illegal removal of grizzly bears from Poll Haven have turned this vital grizzly habitat into dangerous terrain for the great bears. Grizzlies ranging through the adjacent Waterton-Glacier International Peace Park risk death in Poll Haven despite the abundant habitat nearby.

Conservation groups, wildlife agencies and land management planners recognize the critical importance of stopping—or even reversing—the tide of habitat loss that has driven grizzlies out of most of their former North American range. They have begun looking for

Ecocentres

Biologists such as John Craighead use the term "ecocentre" to describe a place where grizzly bears find seasonal concentrations of high-quality food. Salmon streams make natural ecocentres; garbage dumps make artificial ones.

Craighead and his brother criticized the U.S. National Park Service intensely for abruptly closing garbage dumps in Yellowstone in the late 1960s. Their research led them to believe that the abundant food in these artificial ecocentres increased the number of grizzlies that Yellowstone could sustain and kept bears away from recreational areas during the tourist season.

Research has shown that bears with access to dumps or salmon streams grow larger and breed earlier in life than those that wander more widely in search of poorer-quality foods. Nonetheless, garbage dumps are now a thing of the past in the mountain national parks. According to Craighead, the loss of these ecocentres has made Yellowstone's isolated grizzlies more vulnerable.

Recently, Craighead proposed that Yellowstone establish artificial ecocentres—road-killed elk or other food deposited in a few isolated areas in the park. In a book he coauthored with Jay Sumner and John Mitchell, Craighead pointed out that bear habitat around the park is shrinking, not growing, and that bears need all the help they can get. Artificial ecocentres could keep bears away, and safe, from people. They could improve bears' nutritional health and increase the overall carrying capacity of the ecosystem.

Opponents—which include the National Parks Service, other biologists and most conservation groups—argue that artificial ecocentres amount to a tacit admission of defeat. Mainstream conservation efforts remain focused on protecting or restoring wilderness grizzly habitats and increasing human tolerance of the endangered bears in the surrounding landscape. If they fail, however, high-intervention tactics such as Craighead proposes may hold out the last, desperate hope for Yellowstone's isolated grizzlies.

A coastal grizzly fishes for salmon

new ways to protect habitat. Conservation easements, the purchase of development rights and other innovative real estate transactions may keep bear habitat from being subdivided or developed outside parks and protected wilderness areas.

Habitat Effectiveness

There is a deadness about a landscape that should hold grizzlies but doesn't. Something vital is missing. Aldo Leopold described such a place in New Mexico: "Escudilla still hangs on the horizon, but when you see it you no longer think of bear. It's only a mountain now."

Across western North America, many landscapes contain abundant grizzly bear foods, sparse human populations, big wild spaces—but no grizzlies. Some have grizzlies, but far fewer than the habitat could support.

Conservation biologists use the term "habitat effectiveness" to describe how useful available habitat is to wildlife. Effective habitat has few risks and lots of resources. Bear habitat usually loses some effectiveness when people move in because people kill bears. Sometimes the grizzlies move out—just abandon that part of their range.

Much of Banff National Park still looks like good grizzly habitat, but people have made it a dangerous place for bears. Biologists such as Dr. Steve Herrero and Paul Paquet have begun to express grave concerns about the viability of the park's grizzly population. Females with cubs, in particular, regularly come into

Grizzly Foods

What plants do grizzlies prefer? It partly depends on what's available. Biologist Chris Servheen identified 165 plant and animal species that grizzlies eat in just one part of the Rocky Mountains. Some of the most important plants include:

Skunk cabbage (Lysichitum americanum)

Mountain fireweed (Epilobium latifolum)

Dandelion (Taraxacum officinale)

Glacier lily (Erythronium grandiflorum)

conflict with hikers, climbers, roadside photographers and picnickers. Wardens end up trapping and removing them, or shooting them. Grizzlies now completely avoid some areas. Buffaloberries go uneaten each fall; sweetvetch roots grow fibrous and old. Hikers no longer pause in mid-step, shocked into sudden alertness by the sight of long-clawed tracks on the trail.

Most people think of Banff as a protected area, but development has compromised much of it as habitat for grizzlies and other sensitive wilderness animals.

Elsewhere, habitat effectiveness declines when ranchers graze their

The 12% Solution

Canada promised the world that it would set aside at least 12 per cent of its land base by the year 2000 to provide refuge for vulnerable species such as the grizzly bear. Parks Canada, the federal parks agency, has made little headway in meeting this commitment to date, at least in the heavily populated southern parts of the country. Alberta, which made a similar promise, has recently set aside some small areas in grizzly habitat, but it continues to promote development in critical areas such as the West Castle Valley, the upper Oldman and the Swan Hills.

The province of British Columbia, on the other hand, has made exceptional strides in setting aside wilderness. The B.C. government has more than doubled the number of protected areas and parks in the province. These include areas critical to grizzly bears such as the White Grizzly-Goat Range Wilderness, Granby, Khutzeymateen and Tatshenshini.

Gardener of the Wilds

A grizzly's long claws and massive shoulder hump aren't weapons. They're digging tools. Like badgers, pocket gophers and other animals that move a lot of soil, grizzlies have long, slightly curved claws and muscular forelegs.

When a grizzly discovers a good root crop, it may spend several days effortlessly digging it up. It can leave an awesome wake. In Kootenay National Park's Honeymoon Pass, I once found a glacier-lily patch that a grizzly had recently excavated. Rich black soil, like a freshly rototilled garden, covered close to a quarter hectare (half an acre). Along the upper Yarrow Creek valley near Pincher Creek, grizzlies digging for sweetvetch roots left barely any undisturbed ground along almost a kilometre (more than a half-mile) of valley bottom.

Feeding grizzlies leave behind fragments of roots and bulbs that regenerate and produce future crops, much like gardeners dividing perennials. They disturb so much land that they probably play an important role in creating habitat for plants such as dandelion, sweetvetch and strawberry that prefer cultivated seed beds and little competition from other plants.

overleaf: Grizzly bear in a wooded habitat

cattle in grizzly country, or when oil or forestry companies cut roads into remote valleys, enabling poachers to kill bears previously protected by isolation.

Sometimes, agencies or people who care about bears can restore habitat effectiveness. Bear ecologists Wayne McCrory and Erica Mallam, for example, have helped B.C. parks managers relocate campgrounds and hiking trails out of high-quality grizzly habitat to reduce conflict between hikers and bears. McCrory has also teamed up with Dr. Herrero to help Alberta's Kananaskis Country managers make similar adjustments. Many cattle ranchers no longer leave dead cattle in remote pastures where grizzlies might discover them and develop a fatal attraction to beef. Some logging companies quietly lobby provincial governments for the right to close logging roads, partly to protect vulnerable wildlife such as grizzlies.

Banff National Park, however, needs drastic measures to restore its habitat effectiveness, according to the 1996 Banff Bow Valley Study. In the heavily developed Bow Valley, it says that the park must close and remove some tourist facilities, and regulate human use of critical areas.

Moths for Lunch

Steve and Marilynn French observed up to 24 bears at one time, high in the jumbled scree above the timberline in Yellowstone National Park, digging in alpine slopes. The grizzlies were feeding on army cutworm moths that congregate in large numbers in crevices and rubble. Before the discovery, in the early 1990s, biologists had believed Yellowstone's grizzlies fed mostly on whitebark pine seeds during the summer. Since the Yellowstone discovery, biologists have spotted grizzlies feeding on moths as far north as the Waterton-Glacier International Peace Park.

Catch and Release for Grizzlies

When catch-and-release angling became law in Yellowstone National Park, few people realized grizzly bears would benefit.

In 1960, only 3,800 cutthroats spawned in Clear Creek, a tributary of Yellowstone Lake. Thirty years later, with catch-and-release protection, more than 50,000 cutthroats spawn in the same creek in late June and early July.

The fish have become an important seasonal food for grizzlies. Biologists say that the great bears fished in only 41 streams thirty years ago, but now hunt spawning cutthroats in at least 130 streams.

The bounty may soon dwindle, however. In 1995, park authorities discovered, to their horror, that someone had illegally stocked Yellowstone Lake with non-native lake trout. They expect competition and predation to lead to a crash in the cutthroat population. Since lake trout spawn in lakes rather than tributary streams, they will not be available to hungry bears.

What Is a Viable Population of Grizzlies?

A mother grizzly and her yearling cubs

Conservation biologists say that a "viable" population of bears or other animals must have a 95-per-cent statistical probability of surviving for a hundred years. They have built mathematical models to estimate the minimum size of viable bear populations. Models contain assumptions and big margins of error, but the emerging consensus is that a grizzly population must have more than 200 breeding adults to survive a century. Dr. Steve Herrero and Wayne McCrory have calculated that 200 breeding adults mean a total population of 400 grizzlies, since only some bears would be of breeding age at any time. According to Dr. Lee Metzgar, however, a viable population of grizzlies in Montana and Idaho would number at least 2,000 bears.

Small, isolated populations may go extinct for several reasons, particularly:

1. Inbreeding. A small population makes it more likely that related bears will mate with each other. Inbreeding causes abnormalities that can increase the death rate and produce offspring less fertile than their parents.

2. Genetic drift. A small population has a small variety of genes and a higher chance of losing genes when individual bears die. This results in a bear population increasingly different from, and less robust than, the rest of the species.

3. Chance disasters. A major storm, fire, disease or other event that kills a large number of bears can decimate a small population. This isn't a problem where grizzlies from adjacent areas can recolonize the affected area, but it's a big problem for the isolated populations typical of the northern U.S. and southern Canada.

Hunting in Grizzly Country

For some hunters, killing a grizzly ranks as one of the ultimate challenges, just as it always has for some First Nations tribes.

But grizzly bears do not have the biological characteristics of a prey species. They reproduce slowly and occupy huge home ranges. They recover slowly from losses to their populations. As a result, wildlife agencies err on the side of caution in issuing permits for grizzly hunting. Montana, Wyoming, Idaho and Washington no longer allow hunters to kill grizzly bears at all.

British Columbia and Alberta allow grizzly hunting, but only for a few lottery-picked hunters. If a hunter kills a bear, he or she cannot apply for another license for several years. Unlike black bears, it's illegal to shoot grizzly bears over bait.

B.C. hunters kill between two hundred and four hundred grizzlies each year. Alberta hunters kill less than a tenth that number.

Even low-level hunting can still create long-lasting impacts on bear populations—especially if hunters kill mature females. A government review of hunting pressure on grizzlies in B.C. found that hunters killed more than a safe number of grizzlies

Grizzly Dams

A road often spells the beginning of the end for grizzly bears. Grizzlies die regularly on the pavement of Banff National Park's Trans-Canada Highway and Montana's Interstate 17. The World Wildlife Fund has identified Canada's Highway 3, which slices across the Rocky and Selkirk mountains of southern Alberta and B.C., as one of the biggest long-term threats to grizzly populations in northern Montana and Idaho.

Vehicles hit bears on roads. Poachers find bears more easily from roads.

But roads are deadly for a more insidious reason too: they attract development. Uncontrolled development along major roadways results in "grizzly dams"—ecological no-go zones along the valleys that separate the West's mountain ranges. Commercial strips, towns and recreational subdivisions along highways fragment bear habitat.

A single mountain range may support only fifteen to twenty bears. This isn't a problem as long as the bears can travel across the intervening valleys and mate with bears from other mountain ranges.

Once humans take over the valleys, however, grizzlies learn to avoid them, even though valleys usually provide the most productive grizzly habitat. Those that don't often end up dead. Pockets of bears become isolated in less productive high-mountain habitat.

"All these mountain valleys are being developed," says Chris Servheen. "All have these kinds of problems."

Servheen is coordinator of the Grizzly Bear Recovery Team, a group established under the U.S. Endangered Species Act to rescue the grizzly in the Rocky Mountain states. He says that grizzlies face extinction right now, and that Northern Montana, Western Alberta and Southern B.C. will lose in five out of eight management areas, and that the number of females killed exceeded the acceptable level in seven of those areas. Wayne McCrory believes that B.C.'s Wildlife Branch no longer has any excuse for allowing hunters to kill grizzly bears at all.

A controversial 1993 study challenges the idea, prevalent among bear managers, that limited hunting bolsters grizzly populations by removing large adult males and the threat they pose to cubs. Robert Wielgus studied bear populations in Alberta's Kananaskis Valley and B.C.'s Selkirk Range. He concluded that killing adult males may work against the interests of cubs. He says if more young males survive, more young males move into habitat used by females with cubs. The young males, Wielgus suspects, kill as many or more cubs than large dominant males.

But hunting can have an impact on grizzlies even where hunters aren't allowed to shoot them.

In 1995, two hunters failed to return from an elk-hunting trip near Invermere B.C. Searchers sent to find them made an unwelcome discovery. A grizzly and her cubs had appropriated the carcass of an elk the

Grizzly Dams

their grizzly populations if development in valleys continues unabated.

Peyton Curlee, unfortunately, suspects that development will accelerate as baby boomers inherit their parents' wealth. "Trillions of dollars are forecast to pass into the hands of baby boomers in the next 10 years," says Curlee, executive director of the Northern Rockies Conservation Cooperative. "We're forecasting a doubling of subdivisions and recreational second homes as a direct consequence."

Serhveen says: "When we look at the distribution of grizzlies in the northern Rockies [northern U.S.] we see what we see for other carnivores. They extend down in these islandlike, or isthmuslike populations. The low-elevation boundaries don't follow habitat, they follow human development...We've excluded these creatures from their best habitat in most of their North American range."

Further north, the heavily travelled Trans-Canada Highway forms a grizzly dam across the Rocky Mountains in Banff and Yoho National Parks. The town of Banff and its surrounding developments form another dam that blocks movement east and west along the Bow Valley. Recreational real estate development is building more such dams in southern B.C. and Alberta.

Grizzly populations isolated behind these ecological dams will continue to wink out one by one, says Chris Servheen, unless people give bears secure ways to travel through the whole landscape. Most conservation biologists now say grizzlies need large wilderness preserves, connected to one another by secure corridors of habitat, and surrounded with sensitively managed forest and ranching areas.

hunters had shot. The mauled bodies of both hunters lay nearby, along with their guns and gear. Investigating officials killed all three bears. Later that fall, a grizzly killed another hunter further south, and at least three grizzlies were shot by other hunters, ostensibly in self-defence.

At first, hunters and biologists speculated that the B.C. attacks resulted from bears homing in on the sound of gunshots because the

Bears Ignore Boundaries

Parks just aren't big enough to ensure a future for grizzly bears.

Waterton Lakes National Park barely occupies a third of a male grizzly's home range. Even Jasper National Park—15 times the size of tiny Waterton—has few grizzly bears that spend their whole lives in the park. A grizzly bear conservation strategy released by the B.C. government in 1995 states: "Existing protected areas in themselves...may not be adequate for grizzly bear conservation for a number of reasons:

"1. They are not sufficiently large.
"2. They do not, for the most part, contain prime grizzly bear habitat or all of the ecological requirements of a grizzly bear population.
"3. Many were...initially established...to capture scenic or recreational wilderness values."

Crossed Stars

Grizzly populations have dropped from an estimated fifty thousand in 1850 to fewer than one thousand today in the continental U.S.. Canada's grizzly population has declined too, but less dramatically. Most large mammals in North America have decreased in number. Not *Homo sapiens*. The human population of Canada stood at 2.4 million in 1850, when grizzlies still ranged as far east as Regina. By 1950, Canada had seven times as many people and perhaps half as many grizzlies. Today, Canadians number 30 million and the grizzly is threatened throughout most of its surviving range.

Virtual Grizzlies

World Wide Web sites for grizzly conservation:

Vahallas Wilderness Society . . . . http://www.alpinet.net/williams/
spirithome.html
Land Trusts. . . . . http://www.possibility.com/
LandTrusts/
Greater Yellowstone Coalition . . . . http://www.desktop.org/gyc
Idaho Wilderness. . . . . http://www.wild-eyed.org/
Southeast Alaska Conservation Council . http://www.juneau.com/seacc/
seacc.html
World Wildlife Fund Canada. . . . . http://www.wwfcanada.org/
The Bear Den . . . . http://www2.portage.net/~dmid
dlet/bears/index.html

right: Two grizzlies at play

bears had learned to associate gunshots with gut piles and other remains. Ian Jack, president of the East Kootenay Rod and Gun Club, believes bears may attack elk hunters who use new techniques to sound and smell more like elk. Many elk hunters use sophisticated calls that mimic the sounds made by elk calves and female elk. They also douse themselves with scent derived from elk urine. Jack notes that in every recent case where a grizzly has attacked an elk hunter, the hunter had used elk scent. The bears may have mistaken the hunters for prey.

The problem of grizzly bears homing in on the sound of gunshots is old news further south. The U.S. Forest Service controls important grizzly bear habitat around Yellowstone National Park. Besides supporting grizzlies, the national forests contain abundant herds of elk and mule deer that, every fall, attract hunters from all across the country.

Over the years, the forest service has set up regulations to reduce the

Grizzlies and Clearcuts

Logging and grizzly bear conservation can go together. Bruce McLellan studied grizzlies in southeastern British Columbia's Flathead River valley during the 1980s. The whine of chainsaws and the rumble of logging trucks barely disturbed the slumbers of some of the bears. On a few occasions, McLellan found radio-collared grizzlies bedded down within a few hundred metres of logging operations.

McLellan's grizzlies had a few things in their favour, however, that helped them cope with logging. The Flathead Valley is one of the most productive grizzly habitats in the Rocky Mountains. It remains virtually unsettled, with many roadless areas and, south of the international border, the large protected wilderness of Montana's Glacier National Park. And the logging that McLellan observed was a "first pass": loggers removed only a small portion of the available forest.

Further north, loggers have begun their second pass through the headwaters of the Kootenay and Beaverfoot rivers, an area that lies between Yoho and Kootenay national parks. When they have finished, they will have cut well more than half the merchantable timber. The shrinking forest cover, and the growing network of open roads, put the area's grizzlies under more and more stress each year.

McLellan's research has shown that commercial logging in grizzly country reduces habitat effectiveness unless forestry companies physically close and reclaim logging roads as soon as the loggers move on. Otherwise, hunting pressure increases and a growing number of fishermen, huckleberry-pickers and other recreationists take advantage of the new logging roads to penetrate deep into once-remote areas. This displaces bears or, worse, leads to conflicts that result in dead grizzlies.

Montana's Flathead National Forest now requires companies to close and reclaim roads to ensure that most grizzlies can go about their lives without conflict with motorized recreationists.

A grizzly stands to face an intruder

risk of hunters and bears coming into conflict, since most conflicts end with a dead grizzly that the ecosystem cannot spare. The regulations showed their teeth in 1988 when three Wyoming hunters killed a grizzly. They were fined $2,000 each when court testimony showed they had hung elk meat near their tent and low to the ground. Forest Service regulations state that you must hang game meat at least 100 yards (91

Zero Tolerance

B.C.'s Wildlife Branch, through allowing and mismanaging grizzly quotas, has been participating in the process of local extinctions of grizzlies.

There have been many studies by the wildlife branch, private consultants, Parks Canada and others that document very alarming mortality rates near areas where trophy hunting is permitted. The wildlife branch has set quotas for total human-caused mortalities of grizzlies at four per cent. In many areas they are simply allow-

ing those quotas to be exceeded through inaction. A recent study near Kokanee Provincial Park showed that the wildlife branch's management allowed a third of the female grizzlies in the population to be wiped out.

It makes no sense, when the grizzly bear has been listed as vulnerable, to continue to allow trophy hunting of the most slowly reproducing mammal in North America.

Wayne McCrory, B.C. bear ecologist.

Vital Ground

The Vital Ground Foundation's honorary spokesman weighs more than half a tonne and has a commanding presence. Bart is a 600-kilogram (1,400-pound) Kodiak bear who has starred in numerous Hollywood movies. Now, like many celebrities before him, Bart is putting his profile to work in a greater cause.

John Weaver, science advisor to the Vital Ground Foundation, calls Bart an ambassador bear. Bart's trainers—Doug and Lynn Seus of Heber Valley, Utah—work with Weaver and other conservationists to reverse the tide of grizzly-habitat loss on private land in the Northern U.S. and Southern Alberta Rockies, and in B.C.

Private land will have a big impact on the future of grizzlies. The most productive grizzly bear habitat lies in low-elevation valleys that private interests mostly own. Many of the most critical properties have high real estate values

Vital Ground raises money from private donors and philanthropic foundations and enters into partnerships with other groups or agencies to protect private land. Outright purchase is one option, but it's expensive. Like the Nature Conservancy—a larger organization that also spends donated money to protect vital habitat from development—the Vital Ground Foundation prefers to buy conservation easements or buy development rights to keep large blocks of grizzly habitat undeveloped and sparsely settled.

Weaver, who also serves as deputy director of the U.S. Fish and Wildlife Grizzly Bear Recovery Team, says: "Vital Ground will play an extremely important role in saving habitat for the grizzly and other wildlife."

Reduce the Risk of a Grizzly Encounter

- Know where you will likely see bears during the season you hike (but recognize that bears can range almost anywhere). Learn to recognize seasonal bear foods.
- Check with local park or wildlife authorities to find out if bears are likely to be in the area.
- Be alert and read the landscape. Be conscious of the potential for surprising a bear as the vegetation and terrain changes.
- Make noise in places where visibility is poor, so that you don't surprise a grizzly at such close range that it

feels threatened by you. The best noise is an occasional high-pitched yell. That irritating little tinkle of bear bells doesn't carry far enough.
- For the same reason, try to keep the wind at your back. Let any bears in the area smell you before you arrive.
- Carry bear spray and keep it ready to hand.
- If you smell a rotting carcass or see ravens circling, retreat downwind or make a wide detour, shouting frequently. Never approach anything dead.

left: A grizzly's long claws make it adept at digging for roots, vegetation and insects

metres) from camp and no less than 10 feet (three metres) from the ground, for reasons obvious to hunters who know bear country.

Dick Knight, head of the Interagency Grizzly Bear Study Team in the Yellowstone ecosystem, calls hunters who kill grizzlies "woods wimps." An article in *High Country News* quotes Knight as saying, "If they are afraid of bears they shouldn't hunt in grizzly country."

Hunters kill more grizzly bears in "self-defence" than they need to. Too often, naive hunters over-react to bluff charges or to the mere sight of a

White Out

The number-one threat to grizzly bears today is those white areas on the map that represent private lands. All the human activity going on down there will negate anything we can hope to do for grizzlies on public lands, if we don't find a way to bring rampant development under control.

The next 15 years are critical. The Highway 3 corridor in Alberta and B.C. has the potential to cut off U.S. grizzly populations completely. That's a really frightening possibility—large carnivore populations have already seriously fractured in the northern U.S. Rockies. There are incredible rates of development, and the rate is not slowing down—it's accelerating. Most people aren't aware of the impact of what's happening in the valleys on grizzlies and other species.

Chris Servheen, coordinator of the U.S. Grizzly Recovery Team.

A Scarcity of Ancestors

Almost all the grizzlies that now live in the central Canadian Rockies are descended from the same female—evidence of a remarkable genetic bottleneck in the population, says conservation biologist Mike Gibeau.

Gibeau has examined genetic material from more than 30 bears. The population still has a fairly high overall genetic diversity, probably because wide-ranging male grizzlies have bred with local females. But it is lower than other northern grizzly populations and comparable to grizzlies at the very edge of their natural range.

Gibeau points out that this information helps identify the real conservation priorities for the grizzlies that range through Banff, Kananaskis Country and the east slopes of Alberta's Rocky Mountains. His findings suggest that the population cannot afford to lose any females—disconcerting news, since most problem bears killed or relocated in recent years have been female. Since males account for much of the genetic diversity in the population, Gibeau says that land-use planning needs to ensure that male bears can range widely and safely. This would increase the odds of bears from the Banff areas frequently enough to maintain or restore their genetic diversity.

Bears need as many genetic options as possible to keep up with climate change and landscape transitions.

Burn a Grizzly in Your Furnace This Winter

Any thinking consumer can see Mike Sawyer's point. But some Albertans vilify him because they consider any criticism of the oil and gas industry close to treason. Undaunted, Sawyer and other members of the Rocky Mountain Ecosystem Coalition continue to gather information about the impact of petroleum drilling and exploration on Western Alberta's wilderness, and on the grizzlies and other animals that need it. Then they lay the information before regulatory panels, the media and natural gas consumers throughout the Pacific Northwest.

Oil and gas exploration involves cutting temporary roads known as seismic lines across the landscape, oblivious to streams, ridges or bogs. Exploration crews use tracked or balloon-wheeled vehicles to travel the cutlines, discharging blasts of explosive at regular intervals to evaluate the underlying geology.

Companies guard seismic information jealously, so several energy companies often visit the same area. Rob McManus of the Canadian Association of Petroleum Producers says that energy companies cut an average of 63,000 kilometres (39,000 miles) of seismic lines each year. He describes the result as "seismic spaghetti." Most of Alberta's bear country now looks, from the air, as if dozens of whips have flayed it. Seismic lines criss-cross the forest in all directions.

Once a company gets promising results from its seismic surveys, it applies for the right to drill one or more exploratory wells. Wells require more substantial roads than seismic surveys and, if the company finds petroleum reserves, it builds high-quality industrial roads that become virtually permanent features of the landscape. Energy companies have drilled more than 180,000 oil and gas wells in Alberta this century.

Sawyer points to the Shell-Waterton gas field southwest of Pincher Creek as an example of the impacts of incremental gas development. Virtually every creek valley in the area that Andy Russell described in Grizzly Country now has at least one high-quality gravel road and several wells and pipelines. As recently as the fall of 1995, poachers used one of the roads to shoot a grizzly bear that had taken up temporary residence in a large berry patch. Sawyer says such events are inevitable as long as natural gas consumers and governments don't hold the petroleum industry accountable for restoring grizzly habitat and leaving wilderness areas unimpaired by industrial activity.

Canadian regulatory agencies such as the National Energy Board and Alberta's Energy and Utilities Board continue to resist the arguments of Sawyer and other environmentalists. They approve pipeline expansions and gas export permits without fully evaluating the impact of increased petroleum-sector activity on grizzly habitat.

A grizzly explores its home range

bear at close range. A small but growing number of serious high-country hunters now carry pepper spray to improve the odds that both they and the bear can come out of such a surprise encounter alive.

B.C. wildlife authorities may cut short the hunting seasons for elk, deer and other big game so that they end with the end of berry season. Now, these hunting seasons extend into the late fall, after the berries run out and grizzlies need other foods-none richer than carrion. Shorter hunting seasons would likely benefit both bears and hunters.

Staying Alive in Grizzly Country

Writing about the last grizzly killed in Arizona's White Mountains, more than half a century ago, Aldo Leopold said, "It must be poor life that achieves freedom from fear."

Those who travel in grizzly country can never be completely free of fear. Grizzlies can, and do, kill people.

If that bothers you, many hikes offer grizzly-free scenery: Saskatchewan's Cypress Hills, the Colorado Rockies, California's Sierra Nevada or Utah's Uinta Mountains. Leopold's "poor life" is widely available.

You could just stay home. If you get mugged, at least a bear won't have done it.

But fear doesn't have to shut you out of bear country. You can learn enough about grizzlies to travel wisely in the places where they live. A few commonsense precautions, and an informed understanding of how and why grizzly attacks occur, go a long way to converting fear into watchful caution.

Very few grizzly attacks involve a deliberate attempt by the bear to kill or eat its victim. The powerful shoulder hump and long claws of a grizzly—despite their lethal appearance—are not weapons. They are tools for digging grizzly treats: roots, vegetation, insects and rodents.

The large size and long, relatively straight claws of grizzlies make them poorly suited to climbing trees. They also like open country where good climbing trees aren't always in easy reach. Black bears instinctively climb trees when threatened, but grizzlies have to find other ways to respond to danger.

The first line of defence for a grizzly is to bluff the enemy. Startled grizzlies clack their teeth, turn sideways to show their body size, or make sudden, short rushes at their adversary. Bears prefer to bluff than risk injury in a fight.

If bluffing doesn't work, and the stakes are high enough, a grizzly will attack. When are the stakes high enough? When a female grizzly has cubs to protect, when a bear has laid claim to a valuable food source like a carcass, or when a bear feels cornered.

A grizzly attack is a very rare occurrence, but a potentially devastating one. Often the human victim is badly injured or killed, and usually the bear dies too—hunted down and killed. The tragedy takes a toll in human grief and in another bear lost to a dwindling population. Most attacks involve female grizzlies protecting their young. Grizzly populations need their mature, reproductive females. Killing them eliminates all the cubs they might have had and puts their orphans at

Grislier than Grizzlies

Between 1978 and 1994, black bears injured three times as many—and killed four times as many people in B.C. as the more highly feared grizzly. Black bear attacks accounted for nine human deaths and 71 injuries, compared to only two deaths and 27 injuries caused by grizzly attacks. On average, however, domestic dogs kill more people each year than black bears and grizzlies combined.

The Silvertip Next Door

In the north fork of the Flathead River, researchers have found that mostly young grizzly bears use the valley floor near farms and homes. But they don't know how many of those young bears grow up and move back into the high country.

If young grizzlies, which older bears tend to attack, find security near humans, then a low level of human development may benefit grizzly populations, as long as the human community decides to help the bears stay out of trouble.

But if bears succumb to the temptations of garbage and easily killed livestock, or fall prey to poachers, development makes valleys into mortality sinks—a sort of black hole for grizzly bears. This has probably happened in the Flathead's north fork valley, judging from the number of "problem" bears trapped or killed there each year.

right: The first line of defence for a grizzly bear is to bluff the enemy

risk of dying before maturity.

If you surprise a bear at close range, make yourself as nonthreatening as possible. Avoid eye contact, talk in a soft, monotonous voice, and turn your body sideways to project a low profile while retreating slowly from the bear. Don't crouch down or drop to the ground. Climbing a tree can help if you have time to get well up, but sometimes grizzlies defy conventional wisdom and climb trees they aren't supposed to be able to climb.

If a bear bluff-charges, avoid eye-contact and wait. (It should be easy to wait—when bears have caught me flat-footed, my legs have gone rubbery with shock.) Once the bear has salvaged its pride or regained its confidence, it will usually retreat.

If, in spite of everything, a grizzly attacks you, most experts advise lying facedown on the ground, covering your head and neck, and playing dead. Grizzlies focus defensive attacks on the head. Once a grizzly feels you are no longer a threat, he or she will generally retreat. Many people have survived grizzly attacks by playing dead.

Some people carry firearms in grizzly country, where this is legal. But shooting bears can create more problems than it solves. A poorly placed bullet can turn a harmless bluff charge into a deadly attack. In many cases, bears die unnecessarily simply because someone had a gun. Few grizzly populations can afford unnecessary deaths.

In the past decade, a new line of defence has emerged: pepper spray, marketed under such names as Bear

Field and Sissy

Field and Sissy were two young grizzly bears. The community that named them thought, for a while, it could live in harmony with bears.

The bears were born in the late 1980s somewhere in Yoho National Park and soon became familiar sights, feeding with their mother on the avalanche slopes and floodplains near the small town of Field, B.C.

Researchers captured the bear family and fitted them with radio collars, along with eight other grizzly bears ranging through the protected wilderness of Yoho and Kootenay national parks. The biologists hoped to learn the location of the most important bear habitats so that park managers could protect them from too much human use.

Field and Sissy, however, spent a lot of time in and around the town of Field, especially after their mother died in the spring of 1991. Residents would come across the young grizzlies on side streets or along the road out of town. The bears always kept their distance. They ate dandelions and lawn grasses, but caused no trouble.

Then, in 1992, Field happened across a bowl of dog food that someone had left on a back porch. Next he found some food in a compost bin. The familiar cycle had begun. Field moved to the high country around Lake O'Hara and found food in a campground, finally becoming so aggressive that park wardens had to

Away™ or Counterattack™. Pepper spray comes in aerosol cans and is meant to be squirted into the face of an attacking bear at close range. Its active ingredient is capsicum, a natural chemical derivative of red peppers. Capsicum causes instant painful inflammation of mucus membranes in the eyes, nose and mouth, but apparently causes no lasting damage.

Pepper spray is a good investment for anyone who plans to spend a lot of time in bear country. It has proven its worth in many encounters between hikers and bears. To be effective, bear spray must contain at least 10 per cent capsicum and come in a large enough container to permit the user to fire several blasts.

Bears hit with pepper spray virtually always retreat at once.

Irresponsible hikers may think bear spray makes them invincible. It doesn't: you may miss your chance to use spray in time to stop a charge. There is still no substitute for respect, restraint and responsibility.

Pepper spray has one great advantage over firearms: it punishes aggression. A bear that has experienced the shock of running into a wall of pepper spray will probably hesitate to attack another human. Pepper spray, in other words, can keep both humans and bears alive.

That's the whole idea.

Field and Sissy

trap and ship him to remote northern Alberta. There, he raided an industrial campsite and wildlife officers finally killed him.

Sissy became increasingly comfortable around people and vehicles, and took to feeding along the roadside on the Icefields Parkway, a few miles east of town. There she delighted many tourists with her peaceful demeanour and lack of shyness, but her affinity to roads proved fatal. One day she stepped in front of a tour bus and was killed.

In all, eight of the 11 radio-collared study bears, including Field and Sissy, died within three years. Hunters legally killed two, using logging roads to penetrate the once-remote forests west of

Yoho. Poachers apparently got one and two more died of unknown causes.

That rate of mortality, if it reflects the trend in the rest of the population, describes a grizzly bear population on a fast track to oblivion.

The deaths of Field and Sissy particularly troubled the conservation-minded community of Field. When Sissy died, the townspeople held a memorial service for her.

Bruce McLellan, whose extensive research into bears in southern B.C. has influenced many land-use plans and forestry operations, says bears and towns don't mix. He says when people take up residence in the heart of bear country, permanent grizzly losses will surely follow.

Grizzly Sanctuary

In 1994, B.C.'s NDP government announced it would set aside the rugged Khutzeymateen Valley, 40 kilometres (25 miles) north of Prince Rupert, as Canada's first sanctuary for grizzly bears. It created a 443-square-kilometre (171-square-mile) "Class A" provincial park and banned bear hunting from more than 3,000 square kilometres (1,150 square miles) of the surrounding landscape.

The sanctuary didn't come easily. It took biologists, wilderness advocates and environmentalists a decade of lobbying and media campaigns to persuade the B.C. government to leave undisturbed the remote watershed's population of fifty or so grizzlies. Conservationists had long recommended making the Khutzeymateen Valley an ecological reserve because of its grizzlies, salmon and stands of old-growth forest. But the valley was thrown open for clearcut logging in 1986. By 1988, when the valley's fate seemed sealed, conservationists turned up the heat by taking their cause to the international arena.

An election finally saved the Khutzeymateen. The new NDP government promised to resolve B.C.'s land-use conflicts fairly and rationally, rather than in the interests of business alone. The Khutzeymateen's obvious ecological value assured its protection.

Charlie Russell still shakes his head when he thinks how close the bears came to losing their home place: "It seems remarkable to me that it would have taken so long to set aside a sanctuary for these animals that represent the essence of our country."

The Khutzeymateen River drains the glaciers and rugged headwater valleys of B.C.'s Kitimat Range. It flows between steep valley walls clothed in temperate rain forest and spills its waters into a lush estuary at the inland end of a narrow fjord. "Khutzeymateen" is a Tsimpsean First Nations word that translates, roughly, as "sheltered place of fish and bears."

The annual rendezvous of fish and bears has given the place its fame. Each August, schools of chinook, chum, coho and pink salmon that have massed in the fjord begin their annual spawning run through the estuary and up the river. Grizzly bears—treading bear trails so ancient they are permanently worn into the mossy forest floor—converge upon the river mouth to feast on salmon.

Some of the bears weigh more than 400 kilograms (850 pounds), their size attesting to the richness of their coastal environment and the importance of salmon to their diet. The Khutzeymateen's salmon run is precious. Clearcut logging has destroyed many salmon runs in B.C. Slopes denuded of trees do not hold water very well, which leads to erosion and silt-choked spawning beds, and to floods that scour beds clean of their gravel. But the salmon of the Khutzeymateen Valley return each summer to a pristine watershed.

Conservationists knew the battle to save the valley might increase public interest in visiting it. They also knew this posed its own threat to the

Grizzly Sanctuary

Khutzeymateen Estuary

valley's bears. In protected areas where humans have recreational access to grizzly habitat, history has shown that bears come up the losers.

The environmental groups that had publicized the valley developed a carefully controlled, water-based bear-viewing program. When the government gave the Khutzeymateen formal protection, it adopted this plan.

Visitors to the sanctuary sleep on boats anchored offshore to prevent grizzlies from associating humans with food or waste.

Ocean Light, the boat out of which Russell operated, holds eight people. SunChaser, the other tour boat, holds four. "So 12 people is the maximum per day allowed into the area, and that's only for about one month of the year. The rest of the year the bears are dispersed up the valley and in the mountains.

"The country is rugged and the areas where they hang out during other months aren't open to the public. There's no trails and the river is blocked by logjams. So they have it very secluded there."

Russell says visitors appreciate the chance to learn from trained guides. "People who go bear-watching really want to know how to do it. Most people have lost touch with etiquette in the wild and what our actions do to bears and the possibilities of getting in trouble. People really seem to appreciate getting direction in that way."

Wayne McCrory, Erica Mallan and others who fought hard to save Khutzeymateen's grizzlies from industrial development now hope to make this one place where bears can remain unspoiled by contact with humans, while still allowing a limited number of people to learn from them.

Studying Bears

T wo researchers were radio-tracking a large male grizzly in Yellowstone National Park's Hayden Valley one July day in 1984. Occasionally, one of them stopped and held aloft an H-shaped antenna, slowly sweeping it in an arc to pick up the steady beeping of the transmitter on the bear's radio collar.

The beeping grew suddenly fainter as the men picked their way through heavy timber. Generally, the fainter the beeping, the more distant the bear. But in this case, the bear had bedded down behind a large fallen tree and must have muted the signal. As Doug Dunbar and Jim Hayden stepped around the tree, the 1,400-kilogram (650-pound) grizzly exploded into a full charge.

Hayden leaped aside. Dunbar sprayed the bear twice with capsucin spray, which momentarily disoriented it. Then it got its bearings and piled onto him, knocking him on his back and biting at his belly. Dunbar had the presence of mind to spray the bear one more time, full in the face. This time the bear released him and fled.

The Yellowstone encounter marked the first use of capsucin bear spray in the field. It saved the lives of both a human researcher and a wild bear. The incident also underlined the risks of using radio-telemetry to study wild bears.

John and Frank Craighead perfected the use of radio-telemetry for bear research in the 1960s. The Craigheads, working with national park rangers, captured grizzly bears at Yellowstone garbage dumps and fitted them with ear tags, other markings and, as they perfected the technology, radio collars. Early radio collars suffered from frequent battery failure and a more basic problem—since bears undergo great changes in body mass throughout the year, a collar that fits today may simply slide off tomorrow.

Radio-telemetry poses other problems too. Bears have mauled and even killed researchers trying to fit them with radio collars—a process that requires the capture, tranquillization and handling of very large, highly stressed animals.

Bears, too, occasionally die, sometimes from overdoses or accidents while recovering from tranquillizers, sometimes for other reasons.

Wildlife officers had to kill two bears after a study for B.C.'s Coquihalla Freeway. The bears' radio collars, fitted too tightly by inexperienced researchers, were slowly choking the bears to death. In the late 1980s, Alberta wildlife officials also found a bear with this problem. They trapped an old male grizzly after it began killing cattle and discovered it was sick and emaciated because of a radio collar too small for its neck.

left: Two grizzlies forage in high grass

A tagged bear snacks on dandelions

Nonetheless, radio-telemetry studies have provided by far the bulk of the information bear managers and conservationists now rely on. Bears are notoriously hard to study: elusive, sparsely distributed and highly mobile. Radio-telemetry enables researchers to keep tabs on animals they can't see or track.

Over the years, bear research has mostly concentrated on three lines of investigation: conflict between bears and humans, basic bear ecology and conservation biology.

Research to Reduce Conflict with Humans

Scientists can usually find funding to study ways to protect economic interests from bear damage. Some of the research has helped bears, too. Bee farmers used to shoot on sight bears that raided commercial hives—some still do. But research into the use of electric fencing gave farmers a preventive, inexpensive solution. Other research has helped forestry companies reduce the damage black bears do to sapling trees. Studies have demonstrated that bears forage on the trees only for a short period in spring when other foods are scarce. Some forest companies now put out feeding stations to distract the bears until the spring flush of sap is over and other natural foods have become available.

Dr. Charles Jonkel's students at the University of Montana conducted tests on captive bears to find a deterrent that would improve people's chances of surviving bear attacks. Their research helped put bear-repellent pepper sprays on the market.

Bear research doesn't always put bears and researchers in direct contact. The University of Calgary's Dr. Stephen Herrero interviewed survivors of bear maulings and revisited the sites of many maulings to develop a better understanding of the dynamics of bear attacks. His book—*Bear Attacks: Their Causes and Avoidance*—makes sometimes gruesome reading but has gained wide recognition for helping reduce the risks of travelling in bear country.

Studies of Basic Bear Ecology

Bear ecology has supplied the grist for many Masters theses in universities across North America. Over the years, young researchers have pursued radio-collared bears through the forests and wetlands of virtually every national park in North America, studying bears' food preferences and habitat use.

A crisis or controversy sometimes starts the research—the deaths of two young students in separate grizzly attacks one night in Montana's Glacier National Park led to almost a decade of research funding—but the funding grows soft once the newspaper headlines fade from memory.

Such studies usually last two or three years—many management agencies budget on a three-year cycle—long enough to let researchers generate intelligent questions and begin to hint at some answers.

But a real understanding of bear ecology requires long-term studies that last at least five years. For one thing, bear populations have a low reproductive rate and respond slowly to change. For another, bears can show entirely different patterns of habitat use from one year to the next because weather affects the distribution of food over the landscape.

The Craigheads' research in Yellowstone, and the follow-up studies by Dick Knight and the Interagency Bear Study Team, count among the few examples of long-term bear research. The Canadian national parks have nothing equivalent. In the last five years, however, Parks Canada has hired staff ecologists to piece short-term studies into a longer perspective on bear ecology in park ecosystems.

Conservation Biology Research and Modelling

Any bear biologist trying to understand how bears go about their lives must come to grips with the sheer complexity of natural ecosystems. Landscapes are mosaics of many vegetation types, landforms and microclimates. Bears use a wide variety of food sources and bear populations depend on things invisible to human observers—for example, genetic diversity, breeding cycles and mortality rates.

Conservation biology, the latest field of bear-related research, is the science of populations and landscapes. Conservation biologists ask questions about species survival. How many bears does a population need to safeguard its genetic diversity? How much land do bears actually use? How do human land-use decisions affect the quality of a bear's life?

Two new technologies have proved useful tools for conservation biologists: DNA analysis and Geographic Information Systems (GIS).

DNA is like a blueprint for each individual in the world. Every one of our cells contains this blueprint. From traces of blood or tissue, DNA analysis can differentiate species and even individuals of the same species. Bear ecologists use it to identify not only individual bears, but also the relationship among bears. Michael Gibeau analyzed the genetic makeup of grizzly bears in and around Banff

National Park. He looked for similarities in the DNA of different bears to find out which were related. His results show that Banff's grizzlies may have trouble surviving: most of the bears seem closely related, an indication that few are breeding, especially with bears from other areas.

Conservation biology will make more advances as genetic analysis continues to develop. Already, Dr. John Woods of Mount Revelstoke and Glacier national parks is experimenting with a technique for inventorying an entire bear population without ever touching a bear. It uses a mix of high-tech genetic analysis and low-tech barbed wire. Woods and his colleagues set out scent stations baited with fish oil and ringed with a low-slung single strand of new barbed wire. Visiting bears leave tufts of hair, complete with DNA-rich hair follicles, on the barbed wire.

GIS takes advantage of the phenomenal growth in computer technology during the past decade. Biologists can now build huge computer files that contain layers of

Wayne McCrory,...

Wayne McCrory says that he grew up in B.C. "...at a time when there were still prospectors, outfitters, bears and all those frontier sorts of things—Winchester rifles and all that. I grew up with bears and I guess I developed an early affinity for them. I've always been fascinated by them."

In the early 1960s, McCrory was about to embark on a career as a mining engineer "...when I found out there was such a thing as a wildlife biologist." He changed course, choosing to study bears in Jasper and Glacier national parks.

Now 53, McCrory has studied grizzly and black bears in almost every part of B.C. and Western Alberta and has gained recognition as a leading Canadian authority on bear ecology. He is also—no surprise—a determined and successful advocate for wilderness protection.

McCrory teamed up with his sister Colleen and other wilderness advocates in the sixties to form the Valhallas Society. The society first worked to secure protection for the rugged mountains and forests of the Valhallas Mountain Range west of Slocan Lake. It met that objective in 1983 and went on to successfully campaign for the Khutzeymateen watershed, protected in 1992, and the White Grizzly Wilderness, protected in 1995.

"Every one of those is a critical rain forest bear area," says McCrory, "and together they total just under half a million acres [12 million hectares]."

McCrory, however, is far from ready to rest on his laurels. He serves on the B.C. government's grizzly bear science committee and alternates between his roles as professional biologist, who brings the best possible science to grizzly conservation issues, and conservation advocate.

"Only six per cent of coastal temperate rain forest and 7.3 per cent of interior temperate rain forest has been protected so far," he points out. "That means that industry gets well

information on vegetation, soils, slope, aspect, snow duration and countless other habitat variables. In Banff National Park, ecosystem specialist Cliff Whyte has even incorporated information on human-use intensities. A computer analyses all these variables, conducting millions of calculations in a few seconds and generating analyses biologists could never have dreamed of as little as ten years ago.

GIS modelling has helped demonstrate the importance of corridors of secure habitat to enable bears to move through the landscape. It has revealed the impact of roads and clearcuts on bear habitat, and of human recreation on the ability of bears to travel and forage safely. Most GIS systems can plot three-dimensional maps and graphics that illustrate how bears and landscapes interact. These enable researchers to communicate more effectively with land-management agencies and the public.

... Bear Ecologist

over 90 per cent to clearcut."

McCrory says that parks and protected areas risk becoming islands of extinction if not interconnected with corridors of healthy, secure habitat for grizzly bears. To date, he says, land-use plans have failed to do this.

"On the plus side, we've got a large number of new parks. On the minus side, they're logging the hell out of the landscape in between. The provincial government promotes its new forest practises code as the way it's ensuring logging won't harm wildlife. But there are no grizzly bear habitat guidelines in the forest practises code just as there are no guidelines for caribou or other species that need a large amount of unlogged

Wayne McCrory and cameraman Michio Hoshino

forest. When the guidelines were being formulated, the government insisted that they couldn't result in any substantial reduction in the annual allowable cut, so they don't deal with animals like grizzlies."

McCrory now campaigns for a proposed 265,000-hectare (650,000-acre) park—the spirit bear sanctuary—on the central B.C. coast. This wilderness park would protect coastal grizzlies and rare Kermode bears and—in combination with Haida Gwaii National Park, Tweedsmuir Provincial Park and the recently established Kitlope Provincial Park—would preserve a continuous belt of wilderness habitat stretching from the Pacific Ocean into the B.C. interior.

Watching Bears

F inding a bear used to be as easy as a trip to the nearest park garbage dump. Today, parks store garbage in bear-proof containers, truck it to enclosed transfer stations and then haul it to centralized landfills.

When to Go, Where to Go

National parks and the larger provincial parks remain the best places to watch bears, but now you have to find them on their own turf, living like real bears rather than garbage-pickers.

Experienced bear-watchers find bears by looking in the right habitats, which vary from season to season. Watch for bears at dawn and dusk, when they like to move around. Park information centres generally give weekly or daily updates of bear sightings, so checking with information staff can pay off.

The best time of year to look for high-country bears is early spring—late April and May. Snow often lingers in the high country and most animals roam at low elevations and in open areas where vegetation has started to green. You can easily spot bears and other wildlife because most trees and shrubs in bear country don't leaf out until late May. Early spring has other advantages too—roads have little traffic, you can get accommodation more easily than later in the year, and you have better odds of viewing a bear without a bear jam.

Another good time to look for high-country bears is from mid-August through early October, when they again congregate at lower elevations to feed on ripe berries. You'll have a harder time seeing them, however—a bear can spend a long time buried in the dense foliage of a berry bush. Park traffic is also heavier in early fall than in spring.

Late summer and early fall are the best times to watch bears congregate around salmon streams—most Pacific salmon species spawn in the fall.

Where to Go in Western Canada

Canadian National Parks
http://www.worldweb.com/ParksCanada_Banff/parks.html
http://parkscanada.pch.gc.ca/parks/np_e.htm

Jasper National Park
Phone 403-852-4401.
Maligne Valley • Watch for black bears and, occasionally, grizzlies right along the road in April, May and early June. Use binoculars or a spotting scope to scan for grizzlies on the open green slopes overlooking Maligne Lake, especially in April and May or again in October and early November. The same slopes often hold bighorn sheep and mountain goats.
Icefields Parkway • Black and grizzly bears feed along the highway right-

left: An explosive situation: photographers crowd a female grizzly with cubs

of-way from April through June. Black bears concentrate on dandelions while grizzlies dig sweetvetch roots and graze young grasses. Even in summer, this is a good place for an early-morning or late-evening drive. You should also watch the open meadows and forest edges along the floodplains of the Athabasca and Sunwapta rivers. You might get lucky and spot a caribou.

Edith Cavell Road and Highway 93A north of Wabasso Campground • Black bears frequent the road, especially in spring.

Banff National Park
Phone 403-762-1550.

Icefields Parkway near Bow Summit • Grizzly bears have turned up here with increasing frequency in recent years, foraging in the open subalpine meadows along the Icefields Parkway in May and June. In summer, it's worth using binoculars to scan the timberline country along both sides of the valley, especially early in the morning.

Waterfowl Lakes • Black bears often forage on dandelions along the Icefields Parkway in May and early June. They also forage in open areas and forest edges around the lakes.

Cascade and Spray River valleys • The wilderness backcountry of Banff's Rocky Mountain front ranges is important grizzly bear habitat. The bears use avalanche paths, stream floodplains and burned-over forests that have not yet filled in with mature pines. The park seasonally closes some areas to hiking and horse travel to protect grizzlies from disturbance and to reduce the chances of a bear incident.

Yoho National Park
Phone 604-343-6783.

Mount Dennis • Bears sometimes visit the north side of the Ottertail Flats, across the Kicking Horse River from the Trans-Canada Highway. Grizzlies occasionally dig roots and browse in the open avalanche paths just west of the town of Field. The parking lot of the park information centre makes the best place to search for them with binoculars. Spring is best, but in summer you can still catch sight of them at high elevations.

Kootenay National Park
Phone 604-347-9615.

Marble Canyon—Paint Pots • Try scanning with binoculars the open avalanche slope meadows on the west side of the Vermilion River valley in late April and early May, and again in October. Grizzlies, and the occasional black bear, use these open habitats for root digging and browsing on low vegetation.

Hector Gorge-Kootenay Pond • The young pine forests along both sides of the highway contain lots of fallen logs, legacy of a fire that swept Kootenay Crossing earlier in the century. Black bears find ants and grubs in the decaying logs, buffaloberries in the understory of the pine forest, and dandelions and other vegetation along the highway and in the numerous open hollows and wetlands throughout the area. Any time of year is good for spotting black bears early in the morning, but early spring is best.

Waterton Lakes National Park
Phone 403-859-2224.

Cameron Lake • The avalanche slopes at the south end of the lake—parts of which lie in the United States—are important seasonal grizzly bear habitat. You can spot them best by using binoculars to scan across the lake from the parking lot very early in the morning in spring, and during spells of hot sunny weather in summer.

Red Rock Parkway • Black bears and the occasional grizzlies frequent the entire length of this road. Watch the open slopes north of the parkway, as well as the meadows scattered along Blakiston Creek. Bear sightings increase in mid-August during years when the abundant saskatoons bushes along the lower part of the valley produce lots of fruit.

Mounts Sofa and Vimy • A good pair of binoculars or a spotting scope can frequently produce sightings of grizzly bears or their tracks early in the spring. Scan from Waterton village, Linnet Lake or the Chief Mountain Highway.

Mount Revelstoke and Glacier National Parks
Phone 604-837-7500.

Roger's Pass • Early spring is the best season to spot black bears along the highway edges or grizzlies foraging on the open avalanche slopes above the highway.

Pacific Rim National Park
Phone 604-726-7721.
Some local boat-tour operators offer trips to watch black bears along beaches in and around Clayoquot Sound.

Contact numbers for other national parks in western Canada:

Riding Mountain National Park (Manitoba)
Phone 204-848-7275.

Prince Albert National Park (Saskatchewan)
Phone 306-663-5322.

Kluane National Park (Yukon)
Phone 403-634-2251.

Alberta Provincial Parks

Peter Lougheed Provincial Park
Phone 403-591-7226.

Highwood Pass • Grizzlies sometimes use this high-elevation pass that transects a complex of avalanche slopes, old-growth forests and open grassy slopes. These habitats produce roots particularly valuable to grizzlies during spring break-up and again in late fall.

British Columbia Provincial Parks
http://www.env.gov.bc.ca/
Phone 604-387-5002.

Mount Robson Provincial Park
Yellowhead Highway (Hwy 16) and Kinney Lake Road • Late April through early June, black bears often feed on the road rights-of-way.

Bowron Provincial Park
Bowron River • Both grizzlies and black bears use the area. Watch for them especially in September during the salmon run. Several dangerous encounters between canoeists and bears have occurred in recent years, however, and some bear biologists have recommended closing the Bowron canoe route during the spawning runs.

Tweedsmuir Provincial Park
Atnarko River • You can sometimes spot bears during September and October during salmon spawning runs.

How to Watch Bears

There are a few basic rules to ensure proper bear-watching.

1. Show respect.
Stay well back from the bear. Give it plenty of space. Do not approach it, make eye contact or give it any other reasons to feel threatened or nervous. Allow the bear to choose how close it wants to be to you. The golden rule applies here: behave toward the bear the way you would like the bear to behave toward you.

2. Stay safe.
If watching a bear from the road, pull your car well out of the line of traffic and park before concentrating on the bear. Many vehicle accidents happen because of people forgetting the rules of the road when they see a bear. Remain in or beside your vehicle in case the behaviour of less responsible people triggers an attack by the bear.

3. Invest in good binoculars, a telephoto lens or a spotting scope.
Tools that help you enjoy a good view of a bear from a distance will help you resist the temptation to put your safety, and the bear's survival, at risk.

4. Never try to influence a bear's behaviour.
Feeding bears, whistling or shouting at them, trying to herd them into a better position for a photograph and other forms of deliberate harassment are dangerous and disrespectful—and illegal in national and provincial parks. A bear that can behave naturally around humans is a rare and valuable creature. Don't let your behaviour contribute to that bear's ruination.

5. Leave early.
If a crowd starts to gather, or the bear seems influenced by your presence, or the location is unsafe, just leave. If you see a female grizzly with cubs, just leave. Be happy the bear exists and that you are alive and well. Nobody wants to live with regrets. Self-discipline and restraint are valuable virtues for humans in bear country.

6. Consider swapping your camera for a notebook.
Cameras turn three-dimensional, living bears into two-dimensional images. They also tempt their owners to move in closer to fill the frame better. Why not use a notebook instead and record details of the bear's behaviour, what it was eating and the nature of the habitat? Writing down observations leads to a deeper understanding of nature. Taking pictures, on the other hand, reduces your ability to observe detail and contemplate what is really happening.

7. Report problems.
Park officials welcome information about bear sightings, especially observations of females with cubs or of injured or aggressive bears. It's also important to let park or wildlife authorities know about any suspicious-looking behaviour on the part of other people. If you suspect illegal activities, use your notebook to record the details (time, licence numbers, description of suspects, their behaviour, other possible witnesses). Do not intervene. Bear poaching is so lucrative, and the penalties sufficiently high, that some poachers may become dangerous if confronted.

White Grizzly (Goat Range) Provincial Park

Whitewater Glacier Trail • Excellent viewing opportunities for grizzlies, including rare white-phase ones. Foot access only. Travel with caution.

Tatsenshini Provincial Park

Haines Road • Grizzlies regularly use the open habitats between Pleasant Camp and the Yukon border. You can book commercial rafting tours that provide excellent opportunities to view grizzlies in spectacular wilderness surroundings.

Khutzeymateen Grizzly Sanctuary

No public access, but trained guides take parties into this protected area in late spring when grizzlies congregate on tidal flats to feed on sedges. You can book a bear-viewing tour through:

EcoSummer
604-669-7741
Tom Ellison, Ocean Light
604-644-7093, fax 604-224-0828
Dan Wakeman, SunChaser
604-624-5472

Princess Royal Island and the proposed Spirit Bear Sanctuary

http://alpinet.net./~williams/spirithome.html

EcoSummer sometimes offers a limited number of late summer and early fall tours to watch black bears and Kermode bears. See EcoSummer's address above or contact Tom Ellison at 604-644-7093. The indigenous Kitasoo people may offer some tours in the future.

United States National Parks

http://www.gorp.com/gorp/resourc e/US_National_Park/main.htm
Alaska
http://alaskan.com/docs/
http://www.juneau.com/seacc/seac c.html

Denali National Park

Phone 907-257-2646.
You have to book tour vehicles to get access to the core of this park. You can easily see grizzlies and other wildlife in the open subarctic landscape.

Kodiak National Wildlife Refuge

Phone 907-487-2600.
The U.S. set aside almost 7,000 square kilometres (3,000 square miles) in 1941 for this refuge on Kodiak Island to protect bears, salmon and other wildlife.

McNeil River State Wildlife Sanctuary

Phone 907-271-2599.
Congregations of fifty or more grizzlies feed on summer-spawning salmon at a series of waterfalls—North America's largest concentration of grizzlies. The sanctuary strictly regulates the number of visitors to protect bears and humans. Prospective visitors must apply through a lottery that selects around 250 people. Ten go in at a time with a biologist-guide to look at bears that have become highly habituated to the close presence of humans.

Katmai National Park

Phone 907-257-2646.
West of the McNeil River Sanctuary, this area also supports large numbers of bears who fish for salmon in

July. The park has very strict rules of behaviour to ensure that bears and humans are safe.

Glacier National Park
Phone 406-888 5441.

Yellowstone National Park
Phone 307-344-7381.

Suppliers of Bear Spray
Bushwhacker Backpack and Supply Company
Box 4721
Missoula, Montana 59806
USA
Bodyguard Industries Canada
Adelaide Station, Box 398
Toronto, Ontario M5C 2J8
Canada

Conservation Organizations

Organizations that buy or protect critical habitat:
The Nature Conservancy of Canada
794A Broadview Avenue
Toronto, Ontario, M4K 2P7
Vital Ground Foundation
Box 2971
Missoula, MT 59806

National organizations that promote wilderness or habitat conservation:
Canadian Parks and Wilderness Society
1019 - 4th Ave. SW
Calgary, Alberta, T2P 0K8
World Wildlife Fund Canada
90 Eglinton Avenue East,
Suite 504
Toronto, Ontario, M4P 2Z7
Canadian Nature Federation
Suite 520, 1 Nicholas Street
Ottawa, Ontario, K1N 7B7 Canada
Canadian Wildlife Federation
2740 Queensview Drive
Ottawa, Ontario, K2B 1A2

Provincial or regional organizations that promote wilderness or habitat conservation:
The Great Bear Foundation
Box 1289
Bozeman, Montana 59971-1289
greatbears@aol.com
The Valhalla Wilderness Society
Box 329
New Denver, B.C., V0G 1S0
vws@web.apc.org
Alberta Wilderness Association
Box 6398, Station D
Calgary, Alberta, T2N 1Y9
Sierra Club of Western Canada
314 - 620 View Street
Victoria, B.C., V8W 1J6
Western Canada Wilderness Committee
20 Water Street
Vancouver, B.C., V6B 1A4
Castle-Crown Wilderness Coalition
Box 2621
Pincher Creek, Alberta, T0K 1W0
Friends of the Flathead
Box 1359
Sparwood, B.C., V0A 2G0
The Grizzly Project
Box 957
Nelson, B.C., V1L 6A5

Organizations that promote the protection or welfare of bears:
Bear Watch
Box 405
Ganges, B.C., V8K 2W1
Northwest Wildlife Preservation Society
Box 43129, Station D
Vancouver, B.C., V6J 4N3
The Humane Society of Canada
347 Bay Street, Suite 806
Toronto, Ontario, M5H 2R7
Animal Alliance of Canada
221 Broadview Avenue, Suite 201
Toronto, Ontario, M4M 2G3

Organizations that raise funds to compensate ranchers for losses to predators:
The Great Bear Foundation
(grizzly: U.S.)
   Box 1289
   Bozeman, Montana 59971-1289
   greatbears@aol.com

Ecotourism and Bear Education

The Great Bear Foundation
Bears and Ecosystems Field Studies
   (1-800-445-2995)
   Box 1289
   Bozeman, Montana 59771-1289
Trail of the Great Bear
   Box 142
   Waterton Park, Alberta, T0K 2M0
Glacier Institute
   Box 1457
   Kalispell, Montana 59903
The Jasper Institute
   Parks and People, Jasper
   Box 100
   Jasper, Alberta, T0E 1E0
McCrory Wildlife Services
   Box 146
   New Denver, B.C., V0G 1S0
Waterton Natural History
   Association
   Box 145
   Waterton Park, Alberta, T0K 2M0
The Yellowstone Institute
   Field Courses and Nature Study
   Vacations
   Box 117
   Yellowstone National Park,
   Wyoming 82190
Tom Ellison "Ocean Visions"
   c/o 4449 - W.10th
   Vancouver, B.C., V6R 2H8
Khutzeymateen Bear Tours
   Dan Wakeman
   (Sun Chaser Charters)

   Box 1096
   Prince Rupert, B.C., V2C 1L4
Outdoor Bear Safety Courses
   Erica Mallam, Biologist
   Box 329
   New Denver, B.C., V0G 1S0

Government Addresses

Canada
   Prime Minister of Canada
   Ottawa, Ontario, K1A 0H3
Alberta
   Minister of Environmental
   Protection
   Legislature Building,
   Edmonton, Alberta, T5K 2B6
British Columbia
   Minister of Environment
   Parliament Buildings
   Victoria, B.C., V8V 1X5
Saskatchewan
   Minister of Environment and
   Resource Management
   Government of Saskatchewan
   3211 - Albert Street
   Regina, Saskatchewan, S4S 5W6
Manitoba
   Minister of Natural Resources
   Legislative Building
   Manitoba, Alberta, R3C 0V8
Yukon
   Minister of Renewable Resources
   Government of Yukon Territory
   Box 2703
   Whitehorse, Yukon, Y1A 2C6
United States of America
   President of the United States
   Washington, D.C.
Alaska
   Division of Wildlife Conservation
   Alaska Dept. of Fish and Game
   Box 25526
   Juneau, Alaska 99802-25526
Washington

Department of Fish and Wildlife
600 - Capitol Way N.
Olympia, Washington 98501-1091
Oregon
Department of Fish and Wildlife
2501 - SW 1st Avenue
Box 59
Portland, Oregon 97207
Idaho
Department of Fish and Game
Box 25 600-S.Walnut Street
Boise, Idaho 83707
Montana
Department of Fish, Wildlife and
Parks
1400 South 19th Avenue
Bozeman, Montana 59715

Selected Readings

Banci, V. 1995. *Conservation of Grizzly Bears in British Columbia: Background Report.* Victoria: B.C. Ministry of Environment, Lands and Parks. ISBN 0-7726-2540-9.

Craighead, F.C. 1979. *Track of the Grizzly.* San Francisco: Sierra Club Books. ISBN 0-87156-223-5.

Domico, T. 1988. *Bears of the World.* New York: Facts on File. ISBN 0-8160-1536-8.

Gadd, B. 1995. *Handbook of the Canadian Rockies.* Jasper, Alberta: Corax Press. ISBN 0-9692631-1-2.

Herrero, S. 1985. *Bear Attacks: Their Causes and Avoidance.* New York: Nick Lyons Books-Winchester Press. ISBN 0-8329-0377-9.

Humane Society of Canada. 1995. *From Forest to Pharmacy: Canada's Underground Trade in Bear Parts.* Toronto: Humane Society of Canada.

Hummel, M. and S. Pettigrew. 1991.

Wild Hunters: Predators in Peril. Toronto: Key Porter Books. ISBN 1-55013-362-4.

Russell, A. 1967. *Grizzly Country.* Toronto: MacMillan of Canada.

Russell, C. 1995. *Spirit Bear: Encounters with the White Bears of the Rainforest.* Toronto: MacMillan of Canada. ISBN 15501-35953.

Scotter G.W. and T.J. Ulrich. 1995. *Mammals of the Canadian Rockies.* Saskatoon, Saskatchewan: Fifth House Publishers. ISBN 1-896618-55-X.

Thomas, D and M. Enns. 1995. *Grizzly Kingdom: An Artist's Encounter.* Calgary: Detselig Enterprises. ISBN 1-55059-105-3.

Afterword

One July afternoon, I joined a small group of campers for a guided hike with a park naturalist in Waterton Lakes National Park. It was a warm day. An occasional junco trilled sleepily in the forest along the Lineham Trail and the distant sound of cascading waters rose and fell on the down-valley breeze.

We had crossed a grassy avalanche slope and re-entered the pine forest when Vincent stopped and turned to talk to the group. His eyes were on my face when they suddenly focused past me and widened. "There's a bear!" he said.

We turned. Twenty meters away, an old grizzly was plodding up the trail behind us, apparently lost in a daydream. I remember being struck by the sag of her paunch and the way that her lips flapped as she walked. It felt vaguely unreal to see her so near, in the bright light of day, and so seemingly oblivious to our presence.

Vincent and I held our arms high and shouted, trying to make sure she saw us before she got too close. The rest of the group stared, spellbound.

The bear stopped and looked at us. She half-turned, then looked back again. Clearly, she didn't want to change her plans even if we were blocking the trail. She hesitated, weighing her options. Then she stepped off the trail and began to pick her way through the trees. She never deigned to glance at our group as she passed below us, maybe two meters away, and disappeared around a corner.

Suddenly a chorus of children's screams and shouts erupted.

I popped the clip from my can of bear spray and jogged up the trail, expecting the worst. But before I had run more than a few steps, two little girls appeared, followed by two more, then two more—a whole procession of bug-eyed, white-faced twelve-year-olds. They were now singing at the tops of their lungs under the firm direction of four equally shocked teenage councilors.

As the first children passed, one looked up with eyes like saucers, extended her arms, and said, "There was a bear only this far away from me!"

The singing and chatter of young voices faded down the valley. The wind eddied among the trees. Again we could hear the far rush of new-born waters and the faint sounds of birds foraging in the shadows.

Vincent and I called an end to the hike and escorted our excited companions back to the trailhead, talking about bear safety and past encounters and all the things that people talk about when they are still pumped up with adrenaline, suddenly bonded together by a sense of shared danger.

No doubt the little girls had good stories for their parents next time they phoned or wrote home. No doubt their parents told their friends about the close calls their daughters had, just as Vincent's and my hiking companions went home with a grizzly encounter to boast about.

But what had happened, really? A bear had tried to walk up Lineham Creek valley and found the valley full of people. That's all.

Finding herself in a stressful situation, the bear figured out a solution to it and went on about her life. We had created in our own minds all the fear, adrenaline, excitement and frightful possibilities. If circumstances had been different—if we had met the bear outside of a park perhaps—somebody might well have shot her and the story, recounted again and again, would have told of a narrow escape. Probably after a few iterations, the bear would have evolved into a raging, foaming-mouthed killer.

That's what we do to bears. While it remains true that bears attack and kill people, it remains no less true that they almost always choose not to. In our dealings with bears, we focus on our fears and fantasies, not on their reality.

The most dangerous thing about a bear is not its claws, teeth or disposition—it's the way we react to it. When we behave as if bears are tame pets, harmless clowns or frightening killers, we create the situations that lead to danger. We may survive those situations. The bears usually don't.

As the twentieth century draws to a close, we need to learn to respect bears for what they really are, and to see that the choices we make almost always affect bears and other wildlife.

Bears have few choices: they need habitat, they cannot compensate for unnatural mortality, they must forage opportunistically for food, and they are bound to act aggressively when they perceive an imminent threat to their young or a valuable food source.

Humans are similar to bears in some ways—we share, for instance, long life, intelligence, omnivorous habits and a capacity for doing harm to other creatures—but humans differ in that we are blessed and cursed with imagination, we have many choices, and we are capable of ethical restraint.

Past human choices have brought us to a time when almost every bear species in the world is under threat. The choices we make tomorrow will determine the future of the dwindling bear populations that survive today. If we inform those choices with ethical restraint—the kind of restraint that would keep us from industrializing the world's surviving wildlands, demanding unrestricted recreational access to bear habitat, and trying to take more than our fair share from a world that animals like bears must live in too—then bears may have a future.

Index

About the Author

Kevin Van Tighem's roots in Western Canada run deep; his family has lived in this region since 1883. Since he graduated with a BSc in plant ecology from the University of Calgary, he has studied wildlife in various western national parks and protected areas. He has written over 200 articles, stories and essays on conservation and wildlife which have won many awards, including the Western Magazine Award, the Outdoor Writers of Canada Award and the Journey Award for Fiction. He has served on the executive committee of the Alberta Wilderness Association and the Federation of Alberta Naturalists, and has organized two major conferences to promote conservation of rivers and river valleys.

Kevin works as a biologist in Waterton Lakes National Park, where he lives with his wife, Gail, and their three children.

Photography Credits

In the following list, photographs are indicated by page number. When there are two photographs on a page, the top or left photograph is indicated as A and the bottom or right photograph is indicated as B.

Esther Schmidt: Front cover, back cover, 10, 19, 33A, 34-5, 37, 56A, 62-3, 69, 76-77, 84-5, 98, 106, 113, 118-19, 128, 132-3, 142

Dennis Schmidt: back cover inset, 2, 9, 12-13, 14, 25, 30, 33B, 38, 44, 56B, 57, 58, 60, 70, 74, 75, 79, 80, 83, 86, 89, 102-3, 105, 109, 110-11, 116, 121, 125, 135, 140, 146

Dan Hudson: 17, 21

Rick Kunelius: 39

Terry Parker: 42-43, 115

Wayne McCrory: 64, 65, 139

First Light/Michio Hoshino: 92, 96-97

Courtesy of Kevin Van Tighem: 24, 27, 69, 78, 160